ISLINGTON
BORN AND BRED

Also by David Perman

Biography

Scott of Amwell: Dr. Johnson's Quaker Critic
Stranger in a borrowed land: Lotte Moos and her writing

History

Cublington, A Blueprint for Resistance
A New History of Ware, its people and its buildings

Poetry

The Buildings
A Wasp on the Stair
Scrap-Iron Words

David Perman

ISLINGTON BORN AND BRED
A Memoir of Childhood

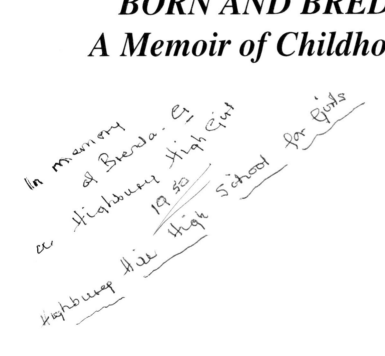

In memory
of Brenda. Et
at Highbury High Girl
1950
High School for Girls
Highbury Hill

Rockingham Press

Published in 2014 by
The Rockingham Press
11 Musley Lane,
Ware, Herts SG12 7EN
www.rockinghampress.com

British Library Cataloguing-in-Publication Data

A catalogue record for this book
is available from the British Library

ISBN 978-1-904851-53-0

Contents

The photos of Lewis Buildings were taken by the late Edward Bowden, who lived there throughout the Second World War. I am grateful to his daughter, Mrs June Hammond, for generously allowing me to reproduce them in this book. I also wish to thank Mavis Ring and John Sanderson, other veterans of the Buildings, for their help. And a big thank-you to Jenny Hyams and Jean Richards who read earlier drafts and made pertinent comments.

1.
The Past is another country

A famous novelist once wrote: "The past is a foreign country: they do things differently there". I really like that. It sums up my feelings about the time when I was growing up in Islington, North London, during and just after the Second World War.

If the past really is a foreign country, you would expect it to have its own language. And that's what we had – a way of speaking recognisably different from today. For 'thank you', we used to say 'ta'. We didn't say goodbye: we said 'tat-ta'. Sometimes we said TTFN standing for 'tat-ta for now' (which came from a popular radio programme, *ITMA*, standing for 'It's that man again'). One of the strangest expressions we used was 'it wasn't half'. If something was *very* good, we would say it wasn't half good – meaning I suppose that if was not half good it must be fully good. This was commonly said in a broad Cockney accent. *'Was the film good? – Yeah, it wernt 'arf'*.

We were all young Cockneys. We came from the part of London which was said to be 'within the sound of Bow Bells' – even though Bow Bells did not ring during the war. Never mind about that! We were born in a part of London which was said to be within the sound of Bow Bells and therefore we were *real* Cockneys. We didn't say 'water' – we said 'wau-a' with a glottal stop (a sort of cough) in place of the 't'. We used to make words like 'I' into a diphthong – something like 'Oy-ee'. When I first took a part in a school play, the master hit me round the head until I pronounced the word 'I' *properly* i.e. without a diphthong. Teachers used to hit boys in those days and there was no ban on 'corporal punishment'. That was partly how I lost my Cockney accent; listening to the BBC where no-one spoke like a Cockney also helped. Only much later – in the nineteen-sixties – did the BBC allow Cockneys, Northerners, Scotsmen and Irish to speak on 'the wireless'. There is a great deal of nonsense written and spoken about Cockney speech. It is sometimes stated that

Cockneys always spoke in 'rhyming slang' – saying, for example, "dog and bone" for phone and "plates of meat" for feet. I can only remember a few examples of rhyming slang from my childhood, perhaps "apples and pears" for stairs and "ball of chalk" for a walk, usually used as a joke by my uncles.

Some of the speech we used was an attempt to be polite. If you had offered my Mum a second cup of tea, she would probably have replied "I won't say no" (in other words, 'yes') or "I don't mind if I do". That expression also came from the radio programme, *ITMA*. We boys also picked up expressions from the radio or from films. If we agreed strongly with something someone had said, we would reply: "you can say that again" or "you're telling me". Or we would use catchphrases from programmes like *ITMA* to get a laugh – phrases like "After you, Claude – no, After you Cecil" or "I'll have to ask me Da'".

Radio was our constant companion. There wasn't any television – well, there was but it was an experiment from a BBC studio in Alexandra Palace. Few people had TV sets and, in any case, it stopped broadcasting when the Second World War began in 1939. Radio on the other hand went on and became more and more important. ITMA finished in 1949 when its star, Tommy Handley, died – he was so much a national figure that our headmaster announced his death in Morning Assembly. ITMA was succeeded by a show called *Much Binding in the Marsh* (about a fictional RAF station) and then in 1951 by the greatest radio comedy of all time, *The Goon Show*. This was the first form of radio surrealism that any of us had heard. We very quickly began to imitate the funny voices and expressions of the characters in the show – phrases like "he's fallen in the water" (from Little Jim, played by Spike Milligan) and "you dirty, rotten swine! You have deaded me!" (from Bluebottle, played by Peter Sellers). Someone described The Goon Show as the first example of verbal cartooning. The Beatles later said that their lyrics had been influenced by the Goons.

Actually, in the period when I was still at school (before 1954) there was no 'pop music' or 'rock-'n-roll' or even a 'youth culture'. That all came from America with the showing of the film, *Rock Around the Clock*, starring Bill Haley and His Comets in 1956 and

The Goon Show, which ran on BBC Radio from 1951 to 1960, starring – left to right – Harry Secombe, Michael Bentine, Spike Milligan and Peter Sellers.

the rock songs of Elvis Presley ('Blue Suede Shoes') and Little Richard ('Tutti Frutti'). There were many other differences. There were no mobile phones, no video games or videos or DVDs. There were no computers or laptops and therefore no Ipads or Kindles. The internet hadn't been invented. Much more basic, there was no plastic – so all my toys were made of wood or metal. Model soldiers were a popular toy – all made of lead, which is considered poisonous and dangerous today. My father bought me a lead model of the Coronation coach in which King George the VI travelled from Westminster Abbey in 1937 – I still have it, though some of the horses have broken legs

There were many other changes. Some of them will appear in the course of this little book. But I think what today's children or teenagers would have found most strange was the way we spoke. We did not use many of today's slang words, like 'cool', 'great' or 'brill' – they mostly came from America and in the 1950s American speech and attitudes were only beginning to be copied here. We used our own peculiar expressions. Instead of goodbye, we said "so long" or "Abyssinia" – standing for "ah be seeing you".

9

2.
And Islington was another place

Islington in the 1940s and 1950s was very different from the smart, fashionable and expensive borough it is today. From the beginning of the twentieth century, the upper middle and professional classes (lawyers, academics, writers and journalists) had been moving to the suburbs to escape the terrible air pollution ('smog'), rubbish-strewn streets and crumbling infrastructure of inner London. The elegant terraces and squares of Georgian Canonbury, Highbury and Bansbury were still there, but they too were run-down, divided into flats and lived in mainly by working-class families or new immigrants. In the 1940s, many Irish, Jewish and other European refugees arrived in the borough, later joined or replaced by Cypriots, both Greek and Turkish speaking, and people from farther afield. It is true that writers like Evelyn Waugh and George Orwell lived at various times in Canonbury square, but they described the area as 'down-at-heel'. The 'gentrification' of Islington began in the 1960s with the arrival of what has been described as the 'camembert classes' (it was said to be impossible to buy a good Camembert cheese in Islington before 1964). It was famously reported that the future Labour Prime Minister, Tony Blair, lived in Barnsbury before 1997 and it was in a restaurant in Upper Street that he and Gordon Brown agreed to share the leadership of a Labour government. The restaurant has now closed and it is reported that the teachers and young lawyers are being priced out of Islington by bankers and financiers, exploiting the good transport links with the City and Canary Wharf.

All that is common knowledge. My main memory of old Islington is of Upper Street, bustling with shops and shoppers (pride of place went to the department store of the London Co-operative Society opposite the Town Hall) but with no estate agents or pavement cafés, and very few restaurants anyway. From the Angel to Highbury Corner, Upper Street was a thoroughfare close to my heart. We shopped at the Co-op and elsewhere in Upper Street: I think Mum bought her underclothes at Bella's. Opposite was a bookshop, where I had an oil painting displayed – and sold! I found out later that it

A tram and two trolley-buses, similar to those that ran along Upper Street and Holloway Road in the 1940s. They were painted bright red, like present-day London buses.

was bought by my Aunt Alice. One of my favourite subjects was the tower and spire of St. Mary's Church, Upper Street (the only part not destroyed in the Blitz) and I was allowed to paint a mural of it in the hall of Highbury School. A little farther west, on Saturdays I cleaned sewing machines for a rag-trade business at the corner of Almeida Street (there was no Almeida Theatre then).

The traffic in Uppper Street was comparatively light and dominated by trams and trolley-buses. There were three tram routes coming from South London to Islington via Westminster Bridge – Nos. 31, 33 and 35. No. 35 came along Upper Street and then up Holloway Road to the bottom of Highgate Hill at the Archway. I remember going by 35 tram to visit Dad's brother, Frank and his family, who lived near Camberwell Green. It was a rocky and noisy journey, especially when the tram wheels squealed on a bend in the rails. We passed the Angel, then went down St. John Street, Rosebery Avenue and Theobald's Road before descending into the Kingsway Tram Subway and emerging on the Embankment under Waterloo Bridge. That part of the journey was exciting – the subway or tunnel evoked all sorts of fantasies. There was a yellow window between the seats and the platform where the conductor stood and Mum told me that looking through that window would make me sick.

The trams were a great inconvenience to other road users, especially cyclists who risked having their wheels trapped in the rails or the gap in the middle where the tram got its electrical power. They were also difficult to board at times. As the tram lines were in the middle of the road, passengers had to walk out through the traffic, hoping that any cars, vans, motorbikes or cycles would stop to let them through. And boarding a tram meant climbing up two steps after queuing in the road.

Equally inconvenient to other road users were the trolley-buses. Two routes – the 609 and 611 – ran along Upper Street and Holloway Road. Trolley buses drew their power from overhead electric wires and the trolley poles would sometimes detach themselves from the wires. This meant that the bus would stop dead in the middle of the road while the conductor extracted a long pole from under the vehicle and used it to push the trolley back on to the wires. As they were electrically powered, trolley buses made little noise except when the brakes were applied with a hissing noise. This could be very frightening to any cyclist who found himself in front of a trolley bus. Trolley buses were replaced by diesel buses in 1961-62. The trams were withdrawn in 1952 and part of the Kingsway subway later became a traffic underpass.

Upper Street was a mile long, so we were told at school, and ever afterwards I have tried to judge distances by how many Upper Streets that might be. That could be difficult because my memories of Upper Street are of the distinct curve it makes after St. Mary's Church before reaching Islington Green and also of its high and low points. It always seemed to me that once you got to Highbury Corner you were going down hill all the way to Dalston Junction or the City of London, via New North Road.

3.
Living near the Canal

I was born in the part of Islington near The Angel. If you imagine a triangle with Islington High Street/Essex Road forming one side, the Regent's Canal forming a second side and New North Road forming the third, then that is where my family lived. Or to be accurate, my mother's family – the Rockinghams. I never knew my great grandfather, Isaac Rockingham, but he was the one who brought the family to Islington: in the 1890s he became the tunnel keeper for the Islington Tunnel, which takes the Regent's Canal under Pentonville Hill from Colebrooke Row to King's Cross. His job was to take the horses over the hill ready to hitch them to the barges at the other end of the tunnel – the barges were pulled through the tunnel by a steam engine. Isaac died in 1902 and it is said his widow, Mary Louisa Rockingham, then became the tunnel keeper.

Isaac and Mary had two sons who both lived near the canal when they married. Isaac Rockingham the younger – 'Uncle Ike' to

My great-grandparents' cottage, as it was in 1902, next to the entrance to the Islington Tunnel in Colebrooke Row.

my Mum – lived with his family in City Garden Row. His younger brother, George (my grandfather) lived first in Provence Street then Baldwin Terrace, which is parallel to the canal at the bottom of St. Peter's Street. They were typical of the working class families you could find throughout London at that time. My Grandad was a big-handed, big-hearted working man, bronzed from working in the open air in all weathers, universally respected and loved. I remember during the war, when I had been cheeky to my mother, he would rise from the table and pretend to take off the broad, leather belt he wore in addition to braces and threaten to give me a beating. Of course, he never did. His job was a lighterman on the Regent's Canal, steering big open barges or lighters from the London Docks to the railway termini of King's Cross, Euston and Paddington – after the war, he would take me the occasional Saturday on the barge from the City Road Basin to Paddington.

His wife, Caroline Rockingham, had a very different personality. If she ever washed my face, she would always administer a couple of hard slaps with her hand and the flannel, which really hurt. Caroline – "Nanny Rock" to us – was a stern, slim woman who had known great loss as a child (though she never gave us the details) and made up for the loss by driving herself and everyone else harder than was reasonable. In the Twenties she managed a chocolate factory and during the unemployment of the 1930s hired out second-hand suits to men looking for work. Her maiden name had been Samuels and some of her children thought she was Jewish. They had six children: the oldest were two boys, George and Harry, then came Jane Caroline (my 'Aunty Jenny'), then my mother Gladys, another boy, Albert, and then the youngest, Louisa (my 'Aunty Lou'). Mum was the cleverest in the family. She passed the eleven-plus examination for a place at a grammar school – the first in the family to do so – but her mother refused to let her go. She had to stay at the local Hanover Street school to be available to look after her younger brother and sister. Gladys left school when she was 14 in 1925 and became a clerk in a large sales office.

My father, Leonard Perman, was always known as 'Jim' because he took after the character of Sunny Jim, a figure in popular

My grandparents, George and Caroline Rockingham, sitting in the garden of 16 Baldwin Terrace with their youngest child, Louisa, after her wedding. Behind (l. to r.) are Albert, Jenny, Gladys (my Mum) and George. Another son, Harry, was absent.

advertisements. He had been born south of the Thames and spent his childhood in an orphanage in Norwood. Later Jim lived north of the river, near his grandmother, Mrs. Bailey. She became the guardian of Jim and his brothers and sisters after their mother died: she lived in Wynyatt Street (between Goswell Road and St. John's Street) and Jim found lodgings nearby at 71 Moreland Street. It was a poor area which was described by the social reformer, Charles Booth, as an area of poverty and "chronic want". In the 1920s, the Moreland Street

Mission provided shelter for the growing army of the unemployed and used volunteers to distribute food and hot drinks. Mum's older sister, Jenny, met her future husband, Alfred Smith, there. And that is where Gladys met Jim. They were members of a growing band of volunteers which included some of their lifelong friends – Albert Wheeler (whose mother was a companion to old Mrs. Bailey) and his future wife, Cissie, and Charlie and Sarah Barratt. They went about as a group on trips to the seaside, to Hampstead Heath or the London parks. In that company, Jim was by far the smallest of the men but was always popular for his charm and his jokes.

They also joined the church and 'took the pledge' as members of the Band of Hope who abstained from alcohol. In later life, Jim would drink the occasional sherry when his children brought it, but Gladys remained true to the pledge. Mum told me that as a child she saw drunks being wheeled home from the pubs on costermongers' barrows (used for selling fruit around the streets). The nursery rhyme 'Pop goes the weasel' includes a verse about going up and down the City Road and in and out the Eagle, which is a pub at the corner of Shepherdess Walk. 'Pop goes the weasel' is thought to refer to men popping or pawning items to get money to spend on drink.

Gladys and Jim were married in 1935 at St. Peter's Church in St. Peter's Street (the church has now been converted to flats). They set up home nearby at 57 Packington Street, where they rented furnished rooms – a living room and a bedroom, with the kitchen, bathroom and toilet shared with other tenants. It was there on 15 February 1936 that I was born. I was delivered by Dr Maddams, an Irish GP whose surgery was in St. Peter's Street. This was some years before the creation of the National Health Service and doctors were paid for visits and medicines, but Dr Maddams had a reputation for undercharging poorer families and overcharging the rich. My birth certificate carried a stamp of King George V, who had died a month earlier. By the time new stamps were printed with the head of his successor, Edward VIII, the new king had abdicated so that he could marry a divorced American woman.

The house where I was born no longer exists. It survived the bombs of the Second World War but was demolished by order of

Jim and Gladys with one-year old David
at Aunt Jenny's house in South Harrow.

Islington Borough Council when it decided in the 1960s that flats were more convenient and modern. Those flats have now been demolished in their turn. That part of South Islington was very different from its appearance today. There were no flats. It was mostly three-story houses with basements and 'areas'. There were few cars about and certainly none parked at the kerbside. And, of course, there were no television aerials or satellite dishes. In winter a pall of smoke hung over the area, often combining with mist and fog to form 'smog', because all the houses were heated by coal fires. Even bedrooms had small grates for fires which did no more than 'take off the chill.' There was no central heating. The streets teemed with people, mostly children, for there were few pre-school or kindergarten places for the under-fives. Hardly any of the houses in this part of London were owner-occupied and most were in multiple occupation. In Baldwin Terrace, my grandparents lived on the ground and first floors of their house – there was another family in the basement and a third family on the top floor.

I do not have many real memories of that period before the war. But the photos Mum kept in the family album help me to recall the past. One of the earliest photos shows me lying in the arms of an unsmiling Granny Bailey – she later pinched me to see if I had the lungs for a good cry, according to Mum. Another photo is of me in a pram outside 16 Baldwin Terrace – there, I was told, I bit off the end of a tin trumpet and poked it into the cheek of Grandad Rockingham. I don't remember that but I do remember looking down Baldwin Terrace from the opposite (western) direction with the iron railings of the houses on my left, the blank walls of warehouses on the right and, at the far end, the gates of an engineering factory. Other photos in the album show a laughing boy with a rather large head in his mother's arms or those of his godmother, Dad's sister Alice Perman, and otherwise engaged in a variety of typical small-child activities – playing with a toy boat in a tin bath at Camber Sands, near Rye in Sussex, riding a tricycle and being posed with a ball or toy in Watson's photographic studio in Seven Sisters Road, near the Nag's Head.

Mention of my Aunt Alice prompts

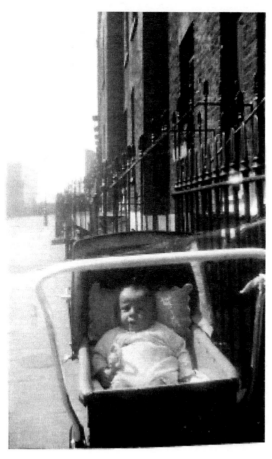

In my pram in Baldwin Terrace, 1936

the story behind another photo in the album. In 1939 she married a Scotsman, named Peter Grice, and I was decked out as the pageboy in a suit of green satin, with lace at the cuffs and neck and white shoes. All would have been well if the wedding photographer had photographed me *after* the ceremony along with the bridesmaids and family. Instead, he singled me out beforehand to pose against a wall and snapped the sweet little boy – who, then, with all the rage that a three-year-old could summon up, ripped the satin jacket and trousers and was led away screaming.

Page boy in green satin

Lewis Buildings, seen from Liverpool Road, in 1910.
They looked much the same in 1939 before the iron railings were
removed as war material.

4.
War is declared

On 2 January 1939, we left Packington Street and moved to Lewis Buildings in Liverpool Road. Jim and Gladys had 'put their name down' on the housing list of the LCC (London County Council) and they were still on that list when they eventually left London in 1955. But a one-bedroom flat in Lewis Buildings was definitely a step up from rented rooms in a private house.

The Samuel Lewis Trust Dwellings for the Poor, as Lewis Buildings were then known, were built in 1910 as the first development of a charity set up by a money-lender, Samuel Lewis. The buildings are still there, though now much modernised and the management company has changed its name to the Southern Housing Group. In 1939 there were five main blocks (A, B, C, D and E), each with three staircases of 20 flats on five floors, as well as F Block which was truncated to fit the diagonal line of Laycock Street. Our flat was No 42 E Block. On the other side of Laycock Street were the much older and run-down Liverpool Buildings (built in the 1860s) where Aunt Alice and Uncle Peter lived. By contrast, the blocks of Lewis Buildings stood like proud galleons, taller than any of the surrounding buildings, with rounded roofs, bay windows and shining bronze-coloured tiles on the staircase entrances and the boundary walls. 42E was a one-bedroom flat and the rent was correspondingly modest: 2s.11d (15p) a week – it was paid in cash at the rent office in F Block. The rent included Venetian blinds on the windows, free chimney sweeping and the use of a drying room with wooden floor slats above heated pipes and with washing lines above.

In 1940-41, the iron railings were removed from the boundary walls as part of Lord Beaverbrook's drive to manufacture tanks from scrap iron. I remember leaning over the railing-less wall to watch Dad cycle off to work down Laycock Street – he wore a brown, corduroy jacket. Another memory of that time was a visit to Chessington Zoo in Surrey, where a clown with a trumpet in each hand marched in front of a band, playing the Grand March from Verdi's 'Aida'.

On the 3 September 1939, Britain declared war on Germany. It was the Second World War which many people had feared would happen ever since Adolf Hitler became the German Chancellor in 1933. I have a memory of standing with Mum outside the Infants' gate of Laycock Junior School, with a label pinned to my coat and a gas mask box hanging by string from my shoulder. The box must have contained a Mickey Mouse gasmask, for I was only three-and-half when war was declared. We were being evacuated and were sent to Northampton, to miserable accommodation with an outside toilet and a pump in the yard for all our water. We stayed there until January or February 1940 when, as nothing seemed to be happening in the war, we came back to London. Lots of families did the same. This was the so-called 'Phoney War' when the Germans concentrated on invading Poland and other East European countries. They did not turn their attention to France and Britain until May 1940.

The Blitz

1940 was a year for which my memories are sharper. We arrived back in Lewis Buildings to find brick shelters being constructed between Blocks A and B, C and D and E and F. They were long and wide with thick concrete roofs and narrow, blast-proof entrances (*pictured below*) – but they were never used. If a bomb had fallen on the Buildings (mercifully it never did) then the flats would have collapsed on to the shelters. Everyone except the Civil Defence authorities knew that. Later the shelters became a public nuisance, inhabited by rats. But at first the whole idea of shelters seemed unreal because nothing was happening in the Phoney War. Yet the authorities were convinced that there would be widespread bombing, particularly of London, and that this would result in hundreds of thousands of civilian deaths. They also believed many of the bombs would release poison gas, which is why everyone was given a gas mask. Air Raid Precautions (ARP) had been drawn up some years before and a network of ARP and fire-watcher centres set up.

Dad – 'Leonard Walter Perman' – became an ARP warden in 1938. His record card (held at the Islington Local History Centre) shows he completed his training and was awarded his silver, buttonhole badge on July 25. When war came, the main purpose of ARP Wardens was to patrol the streets during the 'blackout' to make sure no light was visible to enemy bombers – they also reported the extent of bomb damage and assessed the local need for help from the emergency and rescue services.

They usually wore dark colour overalls and had black helmets with a white W on the front. Dad's record card says he was qualified as a cyclist or motor-cyclist messenger but was also a part-time member of the First Aid party. Under special qualifications, the card reads: *"Disciplined. Able to keep head in an emergency. Guarantee will not desert post intentionally."* What the card does not say is that he was employed at the ARP post in Milner Square, behind Upper Street, where in 1941 he was presented with a cup as the post's table tennis champion. He ceased to be an ARP warden in November 1942 when he was called up for service in the Royal Air Force.

As 1940 wore on, the war came closer to home. First there was the Battle of France which ended in the Dunkirk evacuation of the British Army and some of the French. Then came the Battle of Britain, when the German airforce (the Luftwaffe) tried to take out the RAF fighter defences ahead of a German invasion. By and large the Battle of Britain did not involve the civilian population, but in August 1940, whether by accident or design, the first bombs fell on residential areas of London. But all this was lost on a four-year old boy – or at least hidden from view. There was no television and Mum and Dad were careful not to expose me to news of the war. Besides, the dogfights of the Battle of Britain with Spitfires and Hurricanes taking on the Messerschmitts, Dorniers, Heinkels and Junkers took place over the Channel and near the South Coast and, if there were any over North London, they were hidden by the tall blocks of Lewis Buildings.

But then came the Blitz – the nightly bombing raids on London and other cities which began on September 7 and lasted for 76 nights until May 1941. Bombing in Islington was mainly south of Upper Street but there were 'incidents' (as they were called) in our area. There was a bomb in Barnsbury Park, opposite Lewis Buildings, and a high explosive (HE) bomb fell on the bridge which takes Liverpool Road over the North London Railway, also destroying houses on either side. Mum said that I slept right through all those raids – it probably accounts for my ability to get off to sleep anywhere and at any time. In 1940 Mum and I were the only ones in the flat – Dad was on ARP duty – and I do remember other air-raids when we huddled together in their large double bed, with its tall, dark wooden headboard and base.

There was heavy bombing near the Regent's Canal – probably because the German pilots could pick out the waterway in the moonlight. During the night of September 14/15 there was a raid that directly affected me and my family. The ARP record (at the Islington Local History Centre) gives a matter-of-fact description of what happened:

Incident No. 9 – *Baldwin Terrace/St. Peter's St./Provence St.*

HE bomb penetrated and exploded in gardens at rear of No. 6/ 8 Provence St., causing large crater, demolishing two Anderson shelters and Nos. 4/6/8/10/12/14 Provence Street. Also serious damage to houses in Baldwin Terrace and St. Peter's Street.

There is no mention of casualties but there must have been some. Provence Street backed on to Baldwin Terrace and the map of bomb damage shows that Nos. 1-7 Baldwin Terrace were damaged beyond repair, Nos. 8-12 were seriously damaged and Nos. 13-17 suffered general blast damage. Whether my grandparents were in the house during that night I do not know – they may have been in an Anderson shelter in the garden or in the Angel Tube (Underground) station – but the decision was made to leave London. They had a dog which had to be put down because of cuts to its body and feet from broken glass.

Underground stations were commonly used as air-raid shelters during the Blitz. There are many photographs and indeed films of families sleeping on the platforms, but for me the most evocative scenes are the drawings that the sculptor Henry Moore made of families sleeping in Belsize Park Station on the Northern Line. I am pretty sure that it was in the Angel station that my grandparents sheltered. They came through the Blitz okay. But there was a tragedy at Bethnal Green station, being used as a shelter when, in 1943, a woman tripped on the stairs and 300 people fell and were crushed. My Mum was so affected by that incident that she never again used one of the deep Tube lines and never went on an escalator.

Here we must introduce Albert Rockingham, my mother's youngest brother – he had been called up but then invalided out of the Army because of a weak chest. In 1938 or 1939 he had married a red-headed woman named Ann Russell, who owned an antiques business – really a second-hand furniture shop – in Luton, Bedfordshire. On his release from the Army, Albert trained as a French-polisher to make the furniture more saleable. French polishing is a highly skilled technique of giving wood – especially expensive woods like mahogany – a deep gloss finish. It is now out of fashion because of the application of sprayed on varnishes, but in the 1930s and 1940s it was all the rage. Albert made great play of his new skills and the long time that it took to give an article of furniture a high gloss – I remember him applying the coats of shellac and oil with a *fad* of wadding, making numerous round movements or figures of eight. As a result he had brown fingers which matched his brown hair and moustache.

Anyway, Albert and Annie owned a house on the northern edge of Luton in an area known as Limbury and in November 1940 they began looking around for a house that my grandparents could rent. They found one at 39 Nunnery Lane. Nanny and Grandad moved their furniture there and Mum and I went to live with them before the end of the Blitz – in fact on 21 November (according to my National Registration Identity Card), mainly so that Grandad could, if necessary, sleep at our flat in Lewis Buildings if bombing raids prevented him getting to and from Luton.

5.
Limbury, Luton, Beds

We went to Luton by train – a steam train of the LMS (London, Midland and Scottish Railway) from the old St. Pancras Station. We then took a double-decker bus to Limbury, travelling past Wardown Park and the Commer factory where they used to make vans but were now turning out Bren-gun carriers. The postal address was Limbury, but Limbury was a tiny village with a pub and a few houses – we were going to live in Biscot, which was a suburb of Luton. The house rented by my grandparents – Nanny and Grandad – was in Nunnery Lane. The 'lane' had a post office at one end and a general store at the other and was lined with semi-detached houses, but at the bottom was a working farm, hidden behind a tall redbrick wall. It was only in recent years that I discovered that the farmhouse (now a pub with a carpark where the walled yard had been) was an ancient timber-framed building within its own moat. Beyond the farm was open country and nearby were streets where building had been halted by the war. They had kerb stones laid down and drains, but no pavements or houses yet built.

No.39 Nunnery Lane was cold and damp. Dad said he suffered from rheumatism whenever he stayed there. It was in the middle of a small terrace with a tunnel between it and its neighbour, leading to the back gardens. The roof of the tunnel formed a shelf at the top of the stairs which were always freezing cold, even in summer. Downstairs were three rooms – a back living room where we ate, listened to the wireless (i.e. the radio) and generally lived; this was connected to the kitchen, a long thin room with a door and a high step down into the garden. Here Nanny seemed to be for ever fussing over the gas stove and more often than not burning whatever was in the oven: her baked potatoes were deep brown and hard as Bakelite (a forerunner of plastic). The other room on the ground floor, the 'Front Room', was forbidden territory because it contained all the 'treasures' which Nan had brought from Baldwin Terrace – painted vases, photographs and prints in gilt frames, candlesticks and mysterious, odd shaped boxes. The Front Room also had a piano which I was sometimes allowed to play – strictly on condition that I did not touch anything else in the room.

Upstairs were three bedrooms and a bathroom. The front bedroom was for my grandparents. The large back room was for Mum and Dad when he was with us – it had a large brass bedstead, so old and loose that it rattled like a peel of bells whenever anyone entered the room. The third small room was where I slept – the first room of my own and one that figured in many later nightmares. The bathroom had a gas geezer but no toilet – that was outside in the garden, in a small building up on a concrete platform. The 'lav' had a nine inch gap below the door, which made sitting there in winter a very cold business. Consequently, in each of the bedrooms was an enamel chamber pot or 'po' (as we called it) which went under the bed – though perhaps Nanny's was made of china.

A Village School

On 15 February 1941 I became five years old and the following Easter began school. This was a small village school near the top of Nunnery Lane, next to Holy Trinity Church. It had one large schoolroom and two infant classes would sit there with their backs to each other so that they faced their teachers, who of course could see each other. There was also a Scout hut opposite the church, which I think must have been used for some school activities because that is how I knew the inside. I was much too young to be a Wolf Cub, the equivalent of a modern Beaver Scout. That Scout hut figured in many of my thoughts and dreams – the infants' school less so. In that year, Mum was working as a postwoman and it must have been Nanny who walked me to school. In 1942 we went back to London and when we returned in July 1944 I attended a different school, Norton Road Junior Mixed. I was then eight and was allowed to walk to school alone. It was a longer journey – up Trinity Road, past the Baptist Church (where in 1941 Mum had me dedicated, like the Prophet Samuel) then along Gardenia Avenue to Norton Road. It was near the Baptist Church that a woman came out and violently pushed me off her garden wall, chipping my front tooth, and saying

– when Mum went to protest – that she thought I was one of the boys who had thrown stones at her cat. The tooth remained in its jagged state until replaced by a crown in 2006.

A report of 31 July 1944 from Norton Road school shows that I was in class J7 which, amazingly, contained 59 children. The average age was nine years but I was only 8½. I was given above average marks for most subjects, except Verse Speaking (12 out of 20) and Writing (6 out of 10). Not a good start for a future poet! The class teacher was Mrs D.R. Nelson, a kindly woman in a wheelchair, who remarked at the bottom: "A good report which is the result of good steady work all the term." Under Conduct, she wrote: "V Good indeed". My memories of Mrs. Nelson are warm but I had other feelings about the school. One was being rulered on the hand by a young female teacher, the first time I encountered physical violence.

On 8 March 1942, Mum gave birth to my sister, Jean Gladys. She was born in the Luton and Dunstable Hospital, newly opened in 1939 by Queen Mary in place of an older hospital known as 'the Bute'. Having a little sister was a joy, even though she took up a great deal of Mum's time and attention but it also brought about a change in our lives. Having two children qualified Mum and Dad for a larger flat. When we returned to London in August 1942, we moved into 24B Lewis Buildings, a ground-floor flat in B Block with two bedrooms. So there we were, nicely settled in a larger flat with me having the second bedroom to myself while Jean was still a baby in a cot in my parents' bedroom. By the end of 1942, Dad had been called up in the Royal Air Force (RAF) where he carried on his civilian trade, as a motor parts storeman. It did not look as if we would move again. The war was still on but we British seemed to be scoring some points against the Germans. The D-Day landings in Normandy took place in June 1944 and bombing in London had almost ceased. The war now seemed very distant.

But then came the V1s and the V2 rockets. The V1s – in German the *Vergeltungswaffen Eins* or Vengeance Weapons No. 1 – were the scariest: they were flying bombs whose engine made a noise like a tank until it cut out and the bomb nose-dived to the ground. You would see people in the street looking up when they heard the sound of a V1 or 'doodle-bug' as it was known – when the engine cut out, everyone would dive for cover. The V2 rockets were less scary because you could not hear them coming.

At lunchtime on 27 June 1944, a V1 landed on Highbury Corner, only quarter of a mile from Lewis Buildings. It was not the first in the area – another flying bomb had fallen on the junction of St. Paul's Road and Highbury Grove a few days before, mercifully with only a few casualties. But the Highbury Corner bomb killed 26 people, injured over 150 and caused extensive damage. Eleven Georgian houses in Compton Terrace were destroyed, as well as shops and a bank on the opposite side of St. Paul's Road and the end of Holloway Road. Highbury Station on the North London railway was also destroyed together with the Cock Tavern next to it, and a further row of shops in Upper Street was damaged beyond repair. The damage and the fear of flying bombs sent shock waves throughout London, including in Lewis Buildings. So Mum, Jean and I moved back to Luton where my ID card was registered with 39 Nunnery Lane as my address on 8 July 1944. We stayed there until 8 June 1945, by which time the war in Europe had been over for a month. But Dad was in the Far East with the RAF.

The strange magic of countryside

Our two spells of living in Luton had a special importance for me. It was my first experience of the countryside. Even though the odd status of Limbury as a half-finished suburb of Luton made it less than deeply rural, for me it was a rustic idyll. We did not have to go far on walks with Mum and Dad before we were out of sight of any houses. At the end of Nunnery Lane was a little bridge over a stream, which went by the name of the River Lea, and beyond the bridge was Riddy Lane, which wound its way between high hedges and was barely ten feet across. There would not have been room for two cars to pass but there were very few cars anyway. Riddy Lane was a great place for blackberrying or picking wild flowers.

If, on the other hand, instead of going down Riddy Lane, we had walked straight ahead from the bridge up a sunken cart track, we would pass the bottom of Grosvenor Road, where Uncle Albert and Aunt Ann lived, and from the brow of a hill be able to survey a wide green valley. In the foreground was a field where a German bomber crashed – in one of my poems I said that it crashed in an orchard which then smelled of burnt apples, but that was not true. The crash was in a field and soldiers kept the public well away. But there was an orchard beside the track and once I climbed over the wall and picked up wind-falls. In the distance was Warden Hill rising steeply from the not-so-busy New Bedford Road. John Bunyan, author of the famous *Pilgrim's Progress*, is thought to have imagined Pilgrim progressing over the peaks of this eastern end of the Chilterns. During our earlier stay in Limbury, our walks would sometimes take us on across the road and up Warden Hill to enjoy the amazing views from the summit. Once I had a small sister in a pram and Dad was away in the Forces, such walks were no longer possible.

But having a small sister who took up much of my mother's time did allow me to wander freely in the surrounding fields and paths. I was not exactly a wild child but I did spend many happy hours perched in one of the pollarded ash trees which lined the footpath opposite 39 Nunnery Lane. Hidden among the straight new growth of ash wands, I imagined myself in a ship among the rigging or looking out over the battlements of a besieged castle. There were a few boys of my own age who lived locally and went to the same school and these became my first friends. One was Bobby Barnes who lived in a semi half-way up Nunnery Lane. Together we formed what we called a gang. We would cut down ash wands to make bows and arrows and pretend we were members of Robin Hood's merry band. Once we encountered an older, rival gang which chased us to our houses. They caught me at the end of the passage at No. 39. Before opening the back gate, I turned and received an arrow in the centre of my forehead. I was lucky not to be blinded for the arrow was tipped with a brass bicycle-tyre valve.

Something magical happened because of being in Limbury. For years afterwards, whenever I read a story or heard a story or play on the radio, I imagined that it was set in Limbury. For example, I liked the novels of Thomas Hardy and heard a dramatization of *The Mayor*

The view across Luton from the top of Warden Hill. The valley below was far less developed in the 1940s.

Casterbridge, in which Henchard (the future mayor) gets drunk and sells his wife by auctioning her to a sailor – well, I imagined that happening in Grosvenor Road, opposite Uncle Albert's house. I also liked the novel, *Rogue Male* by Geoffrey Household, in which a man is hunted by German spies and hides underground – well, that I imagined happening in the sunken lane at the bottom of Grosvenor Road. And so on. It was all very strange. But it brought home to me the immediacy of the stories I was reading.

Dad's letters from the war

Dad was called up in the Royal Air Force in November 1942 and after basic training was sent to Iceland. Thereby hangs a tale because Iceland had declared itself neutral at the beginning of the Second World War. However, Britain invaded Iceland in 1941 to keep it out of the hands of the Germans, who had already occupied Denmark, but later in the year British soldiers were replaced by Americans. The RAF still maintained a base for Coastal Command whose aircraft were on the lookout for German U boats and Dad, continuing his peacetime trade as a motor parts storekeeper, served at this base.

But he stayed only a few months.

In June 1943, he was back in Britain and on leave. A photograph in the album – reproduced opposite – shows him in the uniform of a Leading Aircraftman (LAC), standing with Mum, the fifteen-month old Jean with a bow in her hair, and me smartly dressed with a jacket and tie. But again Dad did not stay for long in one posting.

After further training, in early 1944 he embarked at Liverpool on a troop ship for India. This was a journey by way of South Africa and took a long time, from 17 days to a month. After nine days at sea he wrote me a letter, explaining that due to military regulations he could not put a date on the letter or say which ports they had called at. All the same, he managed to fill five pages of fine handwriting and managed to make the letter as entertaining as possible for an eight-year old. He described the porpoises which leaped to and fro in the ship's wake, the pleasure of being able to sunbathe on deck and the concert parties which servicemen put on. By this time Dad was a corporal and his fullest description was of being in charge of a guard party:

> *... they were not really guards in as much as they carried guns – but they were "posted" at various points on the ship to prevent any one not authorised from going to various parts at which they had no business. I mean of course that without anyone to stop them, it is quite possible that some of the boys may find themselves on the captain's bridge, and that would never do because you never know – they might turn the boat around and sail back to England. I for one wouldn't object you may be sure.*

He wished me good luck in the Wolf Cub pack I had joined (it was one attached to St. Mary Magdalene Church in Holloway Road) and reminded me that cubs were junior Scouts and Scouts promised to do a good deed every day – and a good Scout never loses his temper. He signed off with copious kisses – for me, Jean and Mum.

After further training, in the summer of 1945 he was assigned to a task force bound for Singapore and Malaya, which had been occupied by the Japanese since the beginning of the war. From what

A studio photograph taken in 1943, when Dad in RAF uniform was back from Iceland and my sister Jean was fifteen months old.

he told me later, they expected to encounter resistance or at least some gunfire from the shore. But on 6 and 9 August 1945, American bombers had dropped two atomic bombs on the Japanese cities of Hiroshima and Nagasaki and a week later Japan announced its surrender. The formal signing of the surrender instrument was held at City Hall, Singapore, on 2 September. By 26 September, Dad was able to write another letter to me – or this time beginning "Hello Jean & David" – explaining that after camping out on the sand they had left the beach and were now in a town called Kuala Lumpur. Again his handwriting was superb and the descriptions very fine – of tall palm trees with coconuts growing in bunches, of little boys climbing to knock down a coconut in exchange for a cigarette, of houses raised off the ground to keep clear of wet ground and insects. As before, military regulations prevented him saying what he was doing as an RAF corporal in a motor transport unit (MTMU), so he gave his children an exhaustive guide to the insect life of Malaya:

Insects etc are all much bigger than they are in England. The bees are 3 times the size, and what we call cockroaches back there would be small beetles here. There are the usual fireflies, that keep alight flying or settling, they are small though. Then there is the luminous caterpillar, with 40 tiny luminous spots on him, so that at night he looks like a miniature electric underground train going along. There are always lots of lizards at night, probably 3 or 4 in each room, & they climb up the walls & ceilings waiting to catch flies, etc. We do not mind them, as they catch mosquitos, which are small but dangerous if they bite us. There was a moth here last night which I imagined first of all was a bat, as its wings measured nearly 3" across, dark browny colour with a beige line across the wing. I know Alfie would be pleased to get hold of some specimens, but I am afraid it would be rather hopeless attempting to catch them intact & bringing them back over 7,000 miles, wouldn't it? ... There are some nice butterflies, 4 winged dragon flies, some awful looking flying beetles, scorpions and very big spiders about 4" right across from toe to toe (if they have toes).

Alfie was my cousin, Alfred Smith, four years older than me and an amazing collector of everything and anything. Under his bed he kept a large jar of pre-war (i.e. pre-rationing) sweets, which he would bring out every so often to show me – but never to sample! I suppose I must have read the letter to my sister Jean but what she made of the long list of creepy-crawlies I cannot imagine.

Dad later moved to Singapore where he befriended a Malay family who lived in Serangoon Road. While in Singpore, he also met his old friend, Albert Wheeler, who had just been released from Japanese captivity – working on the infamous 'Burma Railway' which figured in the film, *The Bridge on the River Kwai*.

Dad's 'demob' (demobilisation) and return to Britain was delayed by one of the odd episodes of post-war history. In Vietnam, Cambodia and Laos – the former French colonies of Indo-Chna – British forces had taken the surrender of the Japanese and were holding the territory until a new French government was able to take over. As a result, Indo-China was controlled largely from the air and RAF personnel in Asia were kept in place to achieve that. So Dad remained in Singapore until the end of 1946 when he returned home. He was ill with a tropical skin condition and travelled in a hospital ship, where the entertainment was provided by the Music Hall duo, Gert and Daisy, sisters of the actor, Jack Warner. Dad was then demobbed and returned to his pre-war job as a motor parts storeman with G.T. Riches in Store Street, off Tottenham Court Road.

6.
Back in the Buildings

When we returned to London in 1945, the biggest change we noticed was the bomb damage. On the other side of Liverpool Road at the corner of Barnsbury Park, there was a row of ruined houses – we used to play in them, even though it was forbidden by the police and frowned on by Mum and Dad. The bridge carrying Liverpool Road over the North London Line had been destroyed and rebuilt. Most of Highbury Corner had been flattened by the flying bomb in 1944. Elsewhere in London – particularly around St. Paul's Cathedral – there were wide areas of bomb damage. The larger bomb craters had yellow brick walls built around them and were put to peacetime use – either as car parks or, if they were deep enough, emergency water reservoirs for the fire brigade. You can see some of these reservoirs in the black and white films of the period, like *Hue and Cry* and *Passport to Pimlico*.

The area next to Lewis Buildings had the character of a village. In Liverpool Road – between the Buildings and Park Street (now renamed Islington Park Street) – was a terrace of elegant houses with long front gardens. The house nearest the Buildings did not have a garden but instead had a shop in front coming right down to the walkway. This sold groceries mainly and some hardware items for the home. At the other end of the terrace was a pub – the King's Arms – which bore a plaque, saying 'Islington Park Place 1790'. (Most of this terrace was demolished after the war for no good reason – perhaps the same yearning after 'progress' by Islington Council that led to extensive demolition in Packington Street). On the opposite corner of Park Street was a baker's shop, where Mum served for a while, and two doors down was a small newsagent's. On the other side of Park Street was a proper hardware shop, which smelled of oil and camphor and served chopped firewood. I would take the accumulator for our radio there to be topped up with distilled water and recharged – such an accumulator would now be known as a lead-acid battery. Farther down Park Street (on the left) was a fish-

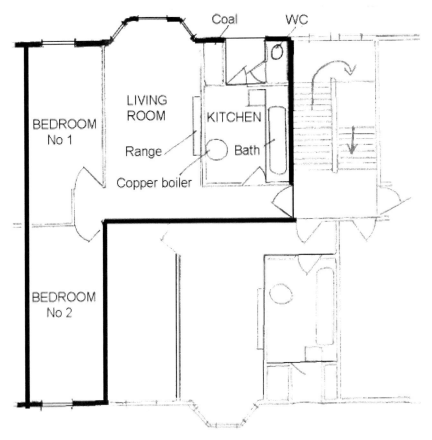

Our flat at 28B Lewis Buildings (No 24B had the same layout). Next door on the landing was No 27B, a one-bedroom flat, similar to the 42E which was our first flat in 1939.

and-chip shop and lower down an up-market butcher's shop.

Our flat was No. 24 in B Block, a ground-floor flat, though later we moved upstairs to No. 28 which was less noisy and admitted less dust. But the layout of the flats was the same. The front door, painted black, was one of four on the landing, reached by a stone staircase. Inside the flat was a passage leading to the living room with a partition of frosted glass on the right and a door leading into the kitchen. But it was not just a kitchen – not by any means! For one thing, it contained a full sized bath, hidden away under a thick wooden table top. When bath night came (usually Friday night – we certainly could not afford more than one bath a week), the table top was lifted up and clamped to a metal hook on the wall. That led to a certain nervousness in case the hook gave way and the table top fell, trapping me in the bath. My sister, Jean, remembers being first in the bath with barely four inches of water and, after the rest of us had bathed, Dad would have twelve inches of tepid and not too clean water. Years later during a period of drought, a Tory minister urged people to share their bathwater – but we had been doing it for years. The water for the bath came from a shiny copper boiler on the other side of the kitchen, which also had a butler's sink, a

Coalmen

gas cooker and cupboards for saucepans and such like. There was no fridge or washing machine, let alone a dish washer.

On the opposite side of the kitchen was another door, which gave on to an open balcony. This served many purposes. It led to the toilet or WC (or 'lav' as we called it – the word 'loo' came much later). On the other side of the balcony was a bank of cupboards. Those at head height were for storing food and had an airbrick in the outside wall; below them was a large coal bunker.

Since all the heating of the flat was from burning coal, we had to have regular deliveries, made by an amazing coalman. He came with a horse and cart, parked in Liverpool Road – it was stacked with open black sacks of coal. He wore a sort of baseball cap, turned backwards, and was covered in black coal dust. But he was an amazing character — he had to be strong and able to move like a dancer. He was also tall enough to stand with his back to the cart and reach up with both hands to pull one of the sacks, weighing a hundredweight (51kg.) on to his back. This he carried from the cart all the way across the yard, up the staircase, through our kitchen and then – by doing a sort of shuffle or dance – he manoeuvred on to the balcony and shot the coal into the bunker. And he hardly ever dropped a lump of coal on Mum's nice, clean floor.

Another dust-covered visitor was the chimney sweep. We had to have the chimneys swept every year and he came with a set of brushes tied in a bundle, which he would then screw on to each other as he thrust them up our range chimney. There were no vacuum suckers, such as sweeps use today. If you were living on the top floor, you could see the sweep's brush coming out of the chimney pot of a flat opposite. Those were the days before the 1956 Clean Air Act, when most people in London burned coal fires. They were the cause of the thick winter fogs or smog (fog combined with smoke).

The living room had a bay window and a range which could have been used for cooking as well as heating the room, but I cannot remember Mum ever doing so. But we did toast crumpets against the fire, using a long metal toasting fork. The living room was choc-a-bloc full of furniture – a leather settee or sofa and two armchairs that Dad had bought back in 1934, an expandable dining table and four upright chairs and a huge oak side-board for china and glasses. The radio and its accumulator stood on a small cupboard against the wall. We did not have a television or a record player. There were few pictures in the living room (I cannot remember any) but there were two or more mirrors. A piano was added much later when I was seventeen and rather too old to learn.

Through an arch hidden by a curtain were the doors to the two bedrooms. Each had a large sash window and a built-in cupboard. The cupboard in the room I shared with Jean – and later with Ray – was stuffed full of old toys and broken furniture. My sister wondered why Dad never put up shelves so that there could be some order among the jumble.

When we first lived in Lewis Buildings, I was much too young to explore the estate or get up to any mischief. But in 1945, aged nine years old, I soon became a member of a gang who all lived in the Buildings and attended Laycock Junior Mixed School in Laycock

Street. There were plenty of opportunities for mischief for the Buildings had lots of hidden places. There were small areas of fenced-off trees and shrubs between all the blocks. Behind A Block was a long garden, mostly overgrown, which was excellent for camps or games of Robin Hood. At the other end of the estate were sheds for residents' bikes, etc. – the top of these sheds were a favourite haunt, particularly as they adjoined the yard of Edwards' engineering works. Our enemy in all these adventures was Hitler – not the Nazi dictator, but the Buildings' supervisor or porter, who had a small black moustache. He had an office next to the 'drying room' where our mothers hung out the 'bagwash' (washing done by laundry firms before the days of coin-operated launderettes). Hitler periodically would go on the prowl and find us climbing on the sheds or making a camp in the shrubberies, and then chase us from one block to another. Once it was we who did the chasing – of a rat, which turned and leapt at me, giving me a fear of the rats as acute as that suffered by Winston Smith in George Orwell's novel *1984*. Our favourite song during these games was:

> *Whistle while you work*
> *Hitler is a twerp*
> *He's half-barmy*
> *So's his army.*
> *Whistle while you work.*

Laycock School

Laycock School was a large, three-storey building, with Infants on the ground floor, Juniors on the middle floor and secondary-school aged girls on the top floor. The senior boys had their own school in Highbury Station Road. Laycock was a spacious school building, with a large assembly hall on each floor sometimes used as a gym and wide classrooms with large windows. I remember being happy there, taking part in plays and concerts or games in the wide playground, which we shared with the senior girls (the Infants had their own playground). I had two spells at Laycock – the first from

Miss Bloomer's class at Laycock Junior School in Spring 1943. I am in the front row (seated, second left).

June 1943 when we first came back from Luton until July 1944, and the second from January 1945 until July 1947. There is a photo of my 1943 class under a teacher named Miss Bloomer: it shows 17 neatly-dressed girls, most with flowers or bows in their hair, surrounded by 21 distinctly rough-looking boys. I am seated cross-legged on the ground, looking just as rough as the boys at the back.

In my second spell at Laycock, I was in the class of a strong-willed, redheaded teacher, named Miss Forward. She was particularly keen on teaching children to do 'real writing' or 'copperplate' (the sort of handwriting my father did so well). My writing was good except in one detail: I formed the letter 'o' with a continuous loop rather than the three strokes – forward, then down to make a circle and forward again – that Miss Forward taught. She had me out at the front of the class and made me copy her movement with the chalk. Twice I did my customary loop and received a smack around the head. The third time I succeeded in copying her strokes and returned to my desk unscathed. I formed a number of lasting friendships at Laycock and when these friends passed the eleven plus exam (known then as 'The Scholarship'), we went on as a group to Highbury County Grammar School. Some of these friends who went from Laycock to

Highbury also lived in the Buildings.

Before my first day at Highbury County, an important event happened. That was the birth of my brother Ray on 22 August 1947. It was I who suggested the name Raymond, after a friend at Laycock who had moved away. The birth took place in 28B Lewis Buildings (home births were more common then). Before her advancing pregnancy made her stop work, Mum had been doing a cleaning job in Belgravia, going out early in the morning, along with Aunt Alice from Liverpool Buildings, to clean for a Mrs Priscilla Phipps while Aunt Alice cleaned for her mother, Mrs Russell Cook. When Ray was born, the two smartly dressed women from the West End came to see Mum and the new baby. I remember them sitting on the edge of the leather settee in the bay window while Mum served them tea. They obviously liked my mother and admired the baby, but what they thought of the ten-year old boy who just stared at them I cannot imagine. Mrs Phipps was married to a lawyer who later became the chief stipendiary magistrate for London. Sadly, she died a year later of polio – poliomyelitis, or infantile paralysis as it was sometime called, a highly infectious viral disease affecting children and young people. A vaccine was developed in the 1950s which led to its eradication – in Britain at least.

Bonding with Dad

When Dad was demobbed in 1946, I was ten years old and almost as tall as him. I soon outgrew him and, as a grammar school boy, moved ahead or at least away from him in other respects. We had not seen much of each other for four years and during that period he had written that I was the man of the family. He said that Mum could look to me for support and I should help look after my little sister. The gap between us was in danger of becoming too wide. It must have been with all this in mind that in 1947-48 Dad made a conscious effort to bond with me. One thing I remember is our Sunday morning trips into the City of London to look at the bomb damage and to explore the ancient financial district. I was surprised that Dad knew so much about the City – he must have worked there at some time –

My brother, Ray, aged 5 in Lewis Buildings

and was delighted with the Wren churches he took me into. I still thank him for my interest in Christopher Wren's London.

Another bonding experience came in October 1948 when the first London Motor Show since the war opened at Earls Court. It was organised by the Society of Motor Manufacturers and Traders, of which Dad's firm, G.T. Riches, was a member. We had tickets to the trade days which happened before the general public was admitted. At that time, the British car industry was rising from the ashes of wartime bombing and the manufacture of tanks and armoured vehicles, and it was doing so with great vigour. The opportunities were wide open. There were few foreign cars on the roads – no Toyotas or Hondas, no Volkswagens or BMWs, few Renaults or Citroëns. On the other hand, all the pre-war British marks were back at Earls Court – Austin, Morris, MG, Wolseley, Riley, Humber, Sunbeam Talbot, Standard, Triumph, Alvis, Rolls Royce, Bentley, Jaguar, Rover and many more. At the 1948 Motor Show many of them were launching new models, including the smart Austin Princess, the dashing Standard Vanguard, the Morris Oxford family saloon and the Minor Minor which was to remain popular for many years. I had a wonderful time, going round the stands collecting the coloured brochures for each new car – which were gladly handed out.

Apart from being together on a day out, Dad and I shared a fascination with cars. He had known and loved them since childhood and, as a motor parts storekeeper/salesmen, he knew their innards as intimately as a surgeon knows a patient's organs. But Dad never owned a car, partly because of poor eyesight, partly because he never aspired to be a driver. I was fascinated by motor cars for different reasons. It seemed to me at that time that all cars had personalities – they certainly had faces with their distinct, round headlights, vertical radiator grills for noses and chrome bumpers for mouths. The Jaguar XK120 with its sleek aluminium body was a beautiful woman, rivalled only by the Aston Martin DB1. The Morris Oxford and its smaller brother, the Morris Minor, were the sort of people you might see coming out of church, whereas the grinning and rather wicked Standard Vanguard would never be seen anywhere near a church. Dad seemed to me to be a Ford Prefect or, better still, a Ford Popular, launched in 1953 – small, reliable and not in the least expensive.

There were other instances of bonding that Dad and I enjoyed in the 1950s. On Sunday evenings, he and Mum attended the Chorley Memorial Hall in King Henry's Walk, off the Balls Pond Road, near Dalston Junction. It was an evangelical mission hall, once linked to the London City Mission, and had what we would now call a Pentecostal form of worship. Services were emotional and uplifting with many cries of 'Amen' and 'Hallelujah' and the singing involved

The 1948 Motor Show at Earls Court

not so much hymns, as in churches, but the choruses composed by the American Ira Sankey for Dwight Moodey's mission to Britain in the 1870s. It just goes to show how old-fashioned worship there was. But Mum and Dad went mainly I think for the companionship of old friends from prewar days, including Cissie and Albert Wheeler – he who had been a prisoner of the Japanese.

At that time Dad – released from the RAF and with more leisure time available – was displaying a talent for making music. He had a good singing voice and an ability to pick up a musical instrument and quickly learn to play it. At home he had a trombone, a couple of bugles or cornets and a motley collection of flutes. Now at Chorley Hall there was the opportunity to acquire a harmonium – one of those small organ-like instruments, powered by a bellows operated with pedals. In 1954 the Hall became the North-East London Gospel Mission and replaced its harmonium with something electrical and, rather than put it on the scrap heap, they let Dad take it away. Or rather Dad and me, with the aid of pram chassis:

'Harmonium'

On a bright June evening with no need of lights
we laboured a pram chassis bearing a load
which wobbled and creaked and hissed out odd notes,
a small whistling man and a tall boy in shorts
pushing a harmonium up Balls Pond Road.

It came from the Gospel Hall where the fat woman
who played it at meetings insisted the need
for something electric which could hold its own
against Hallelujahs and shouts of Amen
in place of the harmonium in Balls Pond Road.

We went over tram lines and felt the load lurch
we passed curious people who stared and smiled
and the grunts of an organ came out of a church
to greet its small cousin up on its perch,
the harmonium pushed up Balls Pond Road.

I knew that once home with patches he'd start
repairing the bellows while playing a chord,
just as he'd patched up the old wooden flute
with a four inch split that had once made it mute,
so the harmonium in Balls Pond Road.

He was no collector, just anxious to play –
I found an old letter after he died
from a piccolo salesman regretting to say
that prison would follow his failure to pay –
the free harmonium in Balls Pond Road.

I outgrew his music, bought records instead
and made enough money so that I could afford
to buy any instrument he ever desired.
But nothing can bring back the concert we shared
pushing a harmonium up Balls Pond Road.

Nineteen fifty-two was a harsh winter and Dad and I used the old pram for another purpose. In Upper Street the tram lines were being taken up, so we collected the tar-covered wooden bricks which lay between the lines, to burn them in the range. Burning coal and fuel like the tar blocks were the reason for the thick fogs or smog we had that year.

As I said, we had no television in our flat or a computer or laptop on which to watch films and, of course, there were no videos or DVDs. But there was the cinema – or rather cinemas, for there were many more then than now. In Luton, I remember being taken by Mum in 1944 to see *Meet Me in St. Louis*, in which Judy Garland sang that catchy song: "Clang, clang, clang went the trolley, Ding, ding, ding went the bell …" So different from the trams and trolley buses in Upper Street. In London we had 'Saturday morning pictures', which I was allowed to go to with a friend and his mum or dad. These were put on at a number of cinemas or 'Picture Palaces' including the Odeon in Upper Street and the Blue Hall on Islington Green, but our favourite was the Gaumont in Holloway Road, just along from the old Highbury Underground station. Saturday morning pictures always followed the same pattern – a cartoon (Mickey Mouse or Tom and Jerry), followed by a short comedy (Charlie Chaplin, Buster Keaton or the Keystone Cops) and a children's newsreel and then the main feature, usually a cowboy film. All this was greeted by deafening screams from two hundred children (not yet known as 'kids' except in America) and preceded by a man playing a spot-lit Wurlitzer organ, which rose up from the floor as we were shown to our seats.

What fascinated me most were the cartoons. Walt Disney was my hero – at least until I discovered that, although Mickey Mouse and Donald Duck were his personal creations, most later characters were produced by a huge army of junior animators. At the time I wanted to become an animator in the tradition of Disney or David Hand. I began to buy Disney comics and copy the cartoon characters – proudly writing on the sheets that I had created them freehand and not by the use of any carbons or tracing paper. I still have the folder of those cartoon years. It is a tribute to the wonderful 1940s output

*My freehand drawings of the Disney characters Willie the Whale
and Ichabod Crane and his horse – the originals are in colour.*

of the Disney studios – before they went in for live-action movies or
created Disneylands in Florida or Paris. What fascinated me in
particular were the vividly imagined minor characters in such films
as *Pinocchio* (1940), *Make Mine Music* (1946) – a musical
compendium, similar to the more famous *Fantasia*. That featured
one of my really favourite characters, 'The Whale who Wanted to
Sing at the Met'. Another favourite was *The Adventures of Ichabod
and Mr. Toad* (1949), featuring the stories by Washington Irving and
Kenneth Grahame (the former told by Bing Crosby). I would spend
hours copying and colouring these cartoon characters. But soon
homework would take over my evenings and cartoons had to be put
aside.

7.
Highbury County

In September 1947 I started at Highbury County Grammar School. It was certainly a cultural shock. For one thing, it seemed so grand compared to the other schools I had been to. The three-storey building on Highbury Grove, built first as a school for missionaries' daughters in 1853 (and later used as a sort of boot camp to subject truants to military-style discipline), seemed to me as imposing as any public school. It also had a house system and I imagined the Victorian villas in Highbury Grove were really the boarding houses where midnight feasts took place, as in *Tom Brown's Schooldays*.

But the greatest shock was to be taught not by women, however strict they were like Miss Forward, but by men. And not young men, but men as old or even older than my father, men whose span of years seemed to stretch back to Victorian times, men who knew something of life and death, including fighting in the First World War. Many of the teachers had been with the school since its foundation in 1922. The shock hit us (some literally) in our first Latin lesson given by Mr L.H.L. Lincoln, who was dressed in what appeared to be a form of 'morning dress' – a dark jacket and waistcoat with a wing-collar shirt, striped trousers and apparently hob-nail boots. Entering the classroom, Mr Lincoln began to write the names of the Nominative, Accusative and other cases on the blackboard and then, immediately, swung round to hurl a blackboard eraser at a boy who was talking. His aim was good. His method, before he taught us any Latin, was to teach us the basic grammar of our own language, English – we had to master that before we were introduced to the beauties of *Amo, Amas, Amat*. Les Lincoln was a remarkable man who also had a mission to introduce us to good music – he played records of Beethoven and Sibelius before Morning Assembly, while we waited in rows for the Headmaster to take the stage. Lincoln inspired a comradely affection in a select band of sixth-formers who did Latin A levels with him and I am sure I got my place at Oxford on the strength of the pen portrait of him I wrote in the entrance exam.

I thrived on the grammar school education provided at Highbury, courtesy of the old London County Council, and on 25 March 1948 received a glowing report, stating that I was first in the top class of my year. 'Excellent' was recorded in Divinity (i.e. Religious Instruction), English and Nature Study, A+ in Geography, Latin, Art and Handicraft, A in History, French and Physical Exercise, B+ in Arithmetic and Algebra and only a B in Music – but that was taught by a woman, Mrs Gauld. My report included congratulations from the Form Master, Mr E.S. Wood, and 'Very good indeed' in red ink from the Head, Mr R.J. Marsh.

How did I achieve this proud position so quickly, in my second term at Highbury? The answer is that I became a swat. At home our flat contained very few books – I can list the main ones as *The Bible*, *Our Island Story* (a popular heroic history of England) and a fat Odhams *Encyclopedia*, probably bought on a special offer in the *Daily Herald*. So the whole idea of studying books and finding answers to questions and puzzles was a novel experience. We were given homework and I worked away at my homework on the kitchen table, to the accompaniment of the music and plays of the Third Programme (forerunner of BBC Radio Three) issuing from a small, plastic-fronted wireless. Another reason for my success was that at that stage I lacked any social life. Those of us boys from Laycock who had gone to Highbury were in 'purdah' so to speak – we had stopped 'playing out' with the other boys, we had school uniforms and were being taught 'to speak proper'. We were no longer little terrors from the Buildings. We were coming to terms with the other boys at Highbury, including a substantial number of Jewish boys who had never 'played out' in the streets and came from homes lined with bookcases. It is significant that this lack of a social life served me well in the first year when I was either first or second in the class. But in the December term of 1948, it was noted that I had slipped back to sixth in the class. The Form Master's comment was "he has ability but apparently he could do better, particularly if he were not so talkative." At last I had a social life.

We were sufficiently poor for me to qualify for most of the free offers and grants then on offer for grammar school boys. These

Highbury County Grammar School, which closed in 1964. The building on Highbury Grove was then demolished and replaced by modern buildings for the comprehensive Highbury Grove School, which have been rebuilt in their turn.

included free school meals (pretty awful, particularly when reconstituted meat – 'spam' – was served or reconstituted potato – 'pom'), free milk at morning break (but all children had their free third of a pint then) and a grant from the LCC towards my school uniform of a cap and blazer. In view of our relative poverty, I was also given a free holiday in the summer of 1948. The school had been evacuated to Somerset during the war years and one of the advantages of being in the country was that the boys could help bring in the harvest. The summer of 1948 was the last of these agricultural camps, in fact the last two – one run by my Form Master, Mr Wood, and the other by the school chaplain, the Rev. E.G. Taylor. Mr Wood's camp was held at Williton, a village a few miles inland from the Somerset coast and the port of Watchet. A large marquee and bell tents were erected on a farm and for two weeks the older boys went out to gather in the sheaves behind the harvester machine. Farming was then less mechanised than today and sheaves of corn really did stand in stooks around the field, later to be formed into haystacks. With another boy, Roy Inglis, I was too young to take part in the harvesting but instead helped in the 'cook house' – washing up, slicing bread for the sandwiches that the older boys took with them or peeling potatoes for the evening meal. Mr Wood and another master, Mr Knowles, had brought their wives and children with them which gave a family atmosphere to the camp. Roy and I slept in one of the bell tents with older boys, who introduced us to some of the folklore of Cockney Londoners – these included some fairly ribald songs and rhymes, recitations of *Eskimo Nell* and, once 'Lights Out' had been announced, an anonymous farting competition! In later years, I went to the camps organised by Mr Taylor at Seaton on the East Devon coast – here again I went free, acting as 'quartermaster' or assistant cook.

The school choir

Another thing I did in my first year was to join the school choir. This was run by the school chaplain and Divinity Master, the Rev. E.G. (Edward Goodrham) Taylor. He was a bear of a man, swarthy and broad with a crew-cut of grey hair, who proudly wore in his lapel the badge of the 'Old Contemptibles' – the soldiers who had first gone to France in 1914 in the British Expeditionary Force, described by Kaiser Wilhelm as "a contemptible little army". In fact, 'EG' had served in the Royal Army Medical Corps as a stretcher-bearer, like the composer Ralph Vaughan Williams – one of his heroes. EG organised two concerts during the school year, one with carols before Christmas and another before Easter, as well as a school service held in a local church at the end of the summer term. The concerts were vastly popular with pupils and parents alike and featured many of EG's favourites – carols by Pretorius and Tchaikovsky or borrowed from David Wilcox's Service of Nine Lessons and Carols at King's College, Cambridge, and in the Easter term songs from the Glasgow Orpheus Choir or from the operas of Gilbert and Sullivan and Rutland Boughton. The father of one of the boys was a professional singer and a sure show-stopper was his rendition of the 'Song of the Flea' by Mussorgsky. EG Taylor's contributed to these concerts by conducting with great sweeps of his arms and a growling accompaniment to some of the songs. The piano was played by Mr Lincoln.

The annual school service was held in Christ Church, Highbury Barn. EG Taylor then appeared in cassock and surplice with the bright green hood of a theology graduate of Leeds University. Some time later – probably in the Winter Term of 1948 – I joined the choir of that Christ Church. I had discovered that I liked singing and other people seemed to appreciate my voice. As a twelve-year-old, I had a good clear treble voice, with the ability to sing in tune once I had learned the part and also to reach High C, two octaves above Middle C. But I had another motive for joining a church choir. It was agreed with my parents that by doing so I could be excused Sunday School which I loathed. The Sunday School I had been attending was in the bowels of Union Chapel in Compton Terrace, opposite the bottom of Laycock Street. Union Chapel is a complex building with a large, round auditorium often used now for concerts, particularly of soul music. But tucked away behind and below the main auditorium is a warren of other rooms, some reached by steep stone staircases. It was in one of these subterranean rooms – or cellars – that the Union Chapel Sunday School was held and I hated the venue almost as much as the infantile presentation of Bible stories. There were of course sermons and Bible stories in Christ Church but these were directed at the adult congregation. Little attention was paid to the choir boys, provided they did not giggle or make a noise with the marbles or whatever games they played during the sermons.

The organist and choirmaster at Christ Church was a nice man, with an upturned nose, named Cyril Smith (a name he shared with a famous concert pianist). From Monday to Friday, he worked as an electrician but at weekends he became a master of the organ console – it was from him that I first heard Bach's *Toccata and Fugue in D minor*. Soon after I joined his choir at Christ Church, Highbury, he said that he was leaving to found a choir at another Christ Church, at West Green in Tottenham, and he invited me and two other boys to go with him. As inducements he said that we would be paid as the leaders of the new choir and would also receive travel expenses. So from January 1949 I began a new routine of travelling to Tottenham for choir practice on Friday evenings and on Sundays for morning and evening prayer. The journey was by the former Northern City Line, which ran from Moorgate to Finsbury Park and is now used by First Capital Connect trains from Hertfordshire. I joined it at the old Highbury station in Holloway Road, changing at Finsbury Park on to the Piccadilly Line for Turnpike Lane. It was usually followed by a mad dash to get to the vestry before everybody else was robed in cassock and surplice. With the choir of Christ Church, West Green, I went to a camp at Heacham in Norfolk, organised by the Royal School of Church Music, and while there we sang services in Norwich Cathedral and Sandringham Parish Church. The latter was in the presence of old Queen Mary, the widow of George V, and after the service she came out and said in a deep, German-accented voice: "Very nice, boys".

Music became very important to me. The first compositions I recognised and liked came via Dad, who was especially fond of Gilbert and Sullivan operas and Sibelius's *Finlandia*. Later, being a member of the school choir enlarged my repertoire to include choral works by Bach, Handel and Henry Purcell – including his marvellous verse anthems, 'Hear my prayer, O Lord' and 'Rejoice in the Lord alway'. Then in the church choir we sang a wide range of anthems and settings, including works by Stainer and Stanford. Not having a record player restricted my knowledge of instrumental music but the Third Programme made up for that gap – and there were the Proms. It was chiefly with Philip (Pip) Blumenthal that I went to promenade in the well of the Albert Hall, listening to the BBC Symphony Orchestra playing Brahms and Schubert under the baton

The choir camp in Norfolk, with the organist,
Cyril Smith (left) and me (second from right).

of Sir Adrian Boult, Sir Malcolm Sargent or the wonderful and under-rated Basil Cameron. Pip Blumenthal was a diminutive and very amusing companion – tragically he committed suicide soon after we left Highbury. There were also operas and ballet at Sadler's Wells, which was easily within walking distance from Lewis Buildings — the Sadler's Wells Ballet (later the Royal Ballet) was there and also the company that later became English National Opera, with whom I first saw Bizet's *Carmen* and Gounod's *Faust*.

If Pip was my music companion, it was with Zvi Jagendorf that I went into the West End for the theatre. And we saw some ground-breaking productions – Shakespeare's *Antony and Cleopatra* alternating with Shaw's *Caesar and Cleopatra*, with Vivien Leigh in the lead of both plays and Laurence Olivier and John Gielgud alternating as her Roman lover. There were also Peter Ustinov's comedy, *The Love of Four Colonels*, with Ustinov as the Russian colonel, and Brecht's *Mother Courage and her Children*, performed by the Berliner Ensemble with Lotte Lenya in the lead. That last performance was in 1956 when I had finished National Service and Zvi was in his last year at Oxford.

For Britain, 1951 was a momentous year. In May there was the opening of the Festival of Britain, marking a hundred years since the Great Exhibition in Hyde Park, and the post-war transformation of the Thames' South Bank, with the cigar-shaped Skylon and the new Royal Festival Hall. I remember going with Dad to see the Dome of Discovery and being amazed at the displays about animals, the North and South Poles and outer space – it was as big and much more ground-breaking for its time than the Millennium Dome in 2000. This was the 'Age of Austerity', there were still fuel shortages and rationing and the Festival of Britain seemed to give some hope for the future. But in October of that year there was a General Election. The Labour Party under Clement Atlee, which had brought in such momentous changes as the National Health Service and nationalisation of the railways and coal mines, was blamed for the shortages and replaced by a Conservative government under the former wartime leader, Winston Churchill.

In the Spring, there was a Highbury School trip to Bruges in Belgium. It was led by the Art Master, Mr W.H. Laurie, and its main purpose was to explore the churches and galleries of Bruges and Ghent and study the paintings of Jan van Eyck and the Flemish School. But we were much more fascinated by Gerard David's painting, *The Judgement of Cambysses*, in which a corrupt judge is skinned alive. There were boys from a number of forms in the party and we stayed at the Hotel Venise du Nord. For this trip, I made a withdrawal of £3 from the Post Office Savings Bank account which Mum and Dad had been paying into since June 1936. Since my birth they had also been paying a penny a week into a life insurance policy and did the same for my sister and brother (though by the time of Ray's birth in 1947 premiums were paid annually, rather than weekly to a collector who came to the door).

Highbury County was very much a soccer school – in later years one of the maths masters, Dennis Lewis, coached the school First XI and also the London Schools XI. Another part-time coach was the Arsenal forward Jimmy Logie. I saw Logie play in 1950 in a home fixture against Derby County, when another of the forwards was Denis Compton, while his brother Les Compton was the main stalwart in the Arsenal defence. The match was played, of course, in the old Gunners Stadium off Gillespie Road, which Dad took me to as part of our 'bonding' years. As well as being a famous England cricketer, Denis Compton also featured on advertisements for Brylcreem, the gooey pomade that Dad and I used to keep our hair firmly in place. Incredibly a later ad for Brylcreem had a jingle saying that girlfriends would "love to run their finers through your hair".

At Highbury, we had to do PE which took place in the gymnasium (the last part of the old school to be demolished) under the stern if not downright sadistic supervision of Mr. Vivian Gage. He also supervised the swimming lessons in Highbury's small covered pool and organised the annual cross-country race at Parliament Hill Fields. Since the school in Highbury Grove was not blessed with playing fields, most sports – and especially football and cricket – had to be played at some distance away. The main playing fields used were at Highhams Park in Walthamstow. Getting there meant two bus journeys, with a change at Dalston Junction.

For boys like me with no aptitude for ball games, the alternative was rowing. This also entailed a bus journey – to Stamford Hill – and then a walk down the sloping streets of Clapton to Springfield Park and the River Lee. Our rowing was organised by one of the history masters, 'Nobby' Knowles, who had rowed at Oxford, probably as a college cox because he was quite a small man. Knowles was a great organiser, as he had to be because the Lee Navigation was busy in those days with barges bringing munitions down from the Gunpowder Works at Waltham Abbey and Small Arms factory at Enfield. "Always stay on the inside of a bend." said Knowles in our first lesson and we could see why when a tug appeared with a string of barges, each one swinging farther out than its predecessor on a bend in the river.

Acting it up

But the main event of 1951 for me was my first appearance in a school play. I had never before given serious consideration to acting, though I suppose I must have taken part in a Nativity Play at Primary School. Mum and Dad had taken us to pantomimes, including some held at the famous Collins Music Hall on Islington Green. I had not seen a serious play unless you count the Christmas production of *Where the Rainbow Ends* – that politically incorrect imperialist fantasy with an appearance by St. George (at which we all cheered) and music by Roger Quilter. But I had no experience of learning a part and going on stage to act before an audience. The opportunity to do so came from our new English master in that year who could not have been more different from the quietly spoken Stan Wood, our Form Master in the first year. The new master was Mr D.C. (Donald Collins) Leech, who had a bald egg-shaped head and a Hitler moustache and introduced passionate emphasis into every lesson or conversation. When not teaching, he chain smoked Senior Service cigarettes. He lived in Chelmsford, Essex, where he was the leading light in an amateur drama group, and he had been producing the annual play of the Highbury School Dramatic Society since the 1930s, though with a break during the wartime evacuation.

The 1951 production was *The Duke in Darkness*, a medieval melodrama by Patrick Hamilton. The programme noted that:

> *Only two of last year's cast are in this production, and one of those only in a walking-on part: our audiences will therefore realise the tremendous effort that these boys have put in to reach such a standard of acting suitable for public presentation.*

The "tremendous effort" had a particular meaning for me because it meant getting rid of my Cockney vowels. Since my days of 'playing out' in Lewis Buildings, I had gone some way to losing my Inner London accent – listening to the BBC had helped – but it seems that I still pronounced the first person singular as a diphthong. In other words I did not say 'I' so much as 'Oy-ee' and this Mr Leech was determined to beat out of me. It was much the same process as that used by Miss Forward to correct my hand-writing, i.e. a clout around the head until I got it right. Once that problem had been resolved, I thoroughly enjoyed being in Patrick Hamilton's melodrama *The Duke in Darkness*. My part was that of a courtier to the Duke, named Voulain. This entailed dressing in doublet and hose, with cocked hat and a sword, and wearing make-up. I was one of the conspirators who assassinated the Duke and disposed of his body. As the Duke was played by Gary (Gabriel) Pearson, a large sixth -former (who later became a

Voulin from *The Duke in Darkness*

founder of the *Universities and New Left Review*) and we had to manhandle his body over a balcony, it was a task that needed careful coordination with my fellow conspirators. Once, instead of lowering Gary, we dropped him on to the mattress behind the balcony and had to look down upon him silently cursing us. The most enjoyable part of the evenings (and the matinée performance for the girls of Highbury Hill School) was the after-performance, when we would get out of our costumes, slap on cold cream and laugh and gossip about the performance as we wiped our faces. Firm friendships were made in that play and those of later years, including Alfred Dance, Anthony Barwick, Patrick Ashton and Fred Reddy who were all in my class – and especially Zvi Jagendorf (then known as Herbert) who played the part of a bearded, old retainer named Broulart.

The 1952 play was *The Guinea Pig by* Warren Chetham-Strode, which in 1948 had been made into a successful film. It tells the story of a working-class boy who is sent as an experiment to a snobbish public school and suffers accordingly. Zvi played the part of the reactionary Housemaster, Lloyd Hartley, who opposes the experiment, while I was the Headmaster who stands to gain from its success. The 'guinea pig' part of the boy whose father is a tobacconist in Walthamstow was played by Patrick Hartigan, another classmate and another 'Boy from the Buildings'. An intriguing feature of this production was the playing of two women by younger boys, particularly as one of them was the romantic lead in the sub-plot, the wooing of Mr Hartley's daughter by a new Master. From that I gained a useful insight into Elizabethan drama in which all female roles were played by boys. This was the last production by Mr Leech before his retirement from teaching.

I had a more prominent role in the 1953 play, *Morning Departure* by Kenneth Woollard, produced by Stan Wood. I was the commanding officer of a submarine which, despite all the efforts of the crew and onshore naval establishments, remains stuck on the bottom of the English Channel. The sets consisted of a number of box-like structures, representing the sub and various offices onshore and in one of these I sat throughout the play, sometimes under the spot lights, sometimes in darkness. It was a claustrophobic experience but the play itself was intended to be claustrophobic. I was reported to have given a suitably heroic performance. "Admirable" said a review in the school magazine. During the matinée for the girls' school, some of the audience were said to be in tears. 1953 was my last Christmas term at Highbury, but not my last appearance for the dramatic society. In 1955, the school play was *Major Barbara* by George Bernard Shaw. The part of the Salvation Army major's stuffy father was played by Bob Thomas but on the day of the matinée he was taken ill with laryngitis. I happened to be home on leave from the Army at the time and was asked to read the part, which I did – apparently without many of the girls, including my sister, knowing that I was not acting from memory.

With so many things going on in my life, I became rather detached from Mum, Dad, Jean and Ray. They went on holiday together to Paignton, while I went to school camps on a different part of the Devon coast at Seaton. At weekends, they went on family outings while I was always rushing off to church services in Tottenham. The time when we really came together was Christmas. It was a tradition among Mum and her sisters that we should all go to Eastcote, near Ruislip, where Aunt Lou lived with her husband, Joe Heaps, and their children, Joseph (a contemporary of my sister Jean's) and Pauline (the same age as Ray). Thither would come Auntie Jenny, the other sister, with Uncle Alf Smith and their children, Alf and Jean, and probably – though not inevitably – Mum's oldest brother, George, with Aunt Nell and Eleanor and George and perhaps the other brothers, Albert and Harry, with Harry's wife, Alice, and children, Pamela and Alan. My grandparents, Nanny and Grandad, would already be there, having arrived from Luton to stay with one of the sisters some days before. It was a gathering of the whole clan and really too much for a small suburban semi to accommodate, but somehow we managed.

We would arrive by Piccadilly Line from Baker Street in the late morning and find Aunt Lou's kitchen already a hot, steam-filled factory of food production. Mum would then put on an apron and join her sisters, while we talked to cousins or admired Uncle Joe's garden and the clever, tent-like structure he had erected to preserve his geraniums from the frost. At three o'clock – on Grandad's orders – we would listen to the Queen's broadcast on the radio. Then, late in the afternoon, Christmas lunch was served. Tables would be put together for the adults and older children and small card tables put up for the younger ones. Eating seemed to go on for ever, with offers of second helpings followed by thirds and even more. There was not much drinking of alcohol. In the evening, there would be the telling of tales, the reciting of family reminiscences and then singing. We all liked commuity singing in those days. The songs were those my aunts and uncles remembered their parents singing – Music Hall songs like 'My Old Man said Follow the Van', 'My Old Dutch', 'Down at the Old Bull and Bush', 'Hello, Hello, Who's Your Lady Friend?' 'I'm Hen-ery the Eighth, I am' and 'Only a Bird in a Gilded Cage' – and Nanny would join in. It was one of the few occasions when I felt my grandmother had a warm heart under her stern exterior.

8.
A sixth-former

I did well in GCE O levels, taking and getting eight subjects –
English Language, English Literature, French, Latin, History,
Geography, Maths and Art – and in September 1952 entered the
Highbury Sixth Form. The subjects I chose for A level were English,
French and Latin – there were no intermediate exams like AS levels
at that time. Classes were held in a small room off the stairs at the
southern end of the building. The room had a long table and chairs
and an upright piano, where Mrs Gauld sometimes gave piano
lessons. The classes were quite informal and modelled on university
tutorials. In keeping with the lax habits of the time, some of the
teachers would smoke – Mr Leech with his Senior Service and Mr
Lincoln with a special brand of roll-ups which he would extract from
a silver box and which would frequently go out because of a lack of
saltpetre.

Our Latin set books were Book II of Virgil's epic poem, the
Aeneid – the description of the fall of Troy – and Cicero's *Pro Milone*,
a speech in defence of a man Lincoln described as one of the greatest
gangsters of the Roman Republic. Leech's main contribution to our
English Sixth Form studies was to immerse us in the poetry of
William Wordsworth, particularly *The Prelude* – the long poem about
his childhood – and to a lesser extent Coleridge. The poem of his we
studied was *Christabel*. Leech maintained that everything written in
the eighteenth century before publication of the *Lyrical Ballads* was
prose, chopped up to look like poetry. Fortunately, we also had the
input of a new master, Dennis Ward, who had studied English at
Oxford University where he had gained a 'half-Blue' in boxing and
consequently was known a 'Punchy Ward'. He had a novel approach
to literature and compared Chaucer's language and treatment of his
subject matter in *The Canterbury Tales* to Raymond Chandler's
thrillers (I used the comparison in my A level paper). In French, we
were taught by the Senior Master, Phillips Howells, with texts by
Corneille and Racine and the Romantic poems of Lamartine, the
two Alfreds – de Musset and de Vigny – and Victor Hugo.

Lewis Buildings decked out with flags and bunting for the Coronation; and little girls dressed in Brownie uniforms.

The Coronation

1953 was Coronation Year and I was one of a group chosen to represent Islington schools in the stands on the Victoria Embankment. There were 30,000 schoolchildren in the stands and we made a great noise. It was a cool, overcast morning, despite being the beginning of June, and we had to be in place by 7 am which meant that we left our rendezvous in Islington at around 5.30 am. As Queen Elizabeth was not due to pass our stand until approximately 10.45 am, that meant a very long wait – cheering and stamping our feet were the best ways to keep ourselves occupied. Soon after 8 am things began to happen. First there was the Lord Mayor's Procession from the City of London, then another for the Speaker of the House of Commons, followed by motor car processions of royals, foreign dignitaries, and others whom we could not make out. The large Queen of Tonga was not one of these – everyone seemed to know who she was. Then came the armed services and their bands – numerous bands of the Irish and Welsh Guards, the Royal Marines, the infantry, police and others, including pipe bands from Scottish and Irish regiments, the Gurkhas and the Pakistani Army. At last came the Queen's own procession and Her Majesty with Prince Philip in the glass coach. I had a model of a glass coach at home in a long cardboard box but the real thing was much better.

We schoolchildren on the Embankment did not see the actual Coronation, of course. But others did. It was televised for the first time and twenty million people were said to have watched it, including Mum, Dad, Jean and Ray who went to a neighbour's flat as we did not have a set. We children on the Embankment saw the returning processions after the ceremony and were allowed to leave the stands at about 5 pm. I did not return home immediately but – feeling able to look after myself as a seventeen-year old – went into the West End with a few friends and joined the crowds. In Piccadilly Circus, we watched smartly dressed people getting drunk outside the Criterion Theatre, women from the ATS and WAAF kissing anyone who came within reach (we tried not to) and kilted soldiers climbing lamp-posts and demonstrating that they did not wear anything beneath their tartans. We walked home, arriving after sunrise. I had a paper round to do and duly collected my sack of newspapers from Canonbury Lane. It was only after I had finished delivering that I learned that Dad had been worried at my failure to return from the Coronation and had been down to the paper shop.

But that was not our first night-time jaunt. The previous year, Philip (Pip) Blumenthal and I went to a party, given in Soho by students at St. Martin's School of Art. There had been some talk when I was in the Lower Sixth of my going to art school if I failed to secure a place at university and the art master, Bill Laurie, had recommended St. Martin's. Mr Laurie was gay, all of us boys knew that, so Pip and I knew what we were getting into when we accepted his invitation to the St. Martin's party. It began in the art school in Charing Cross Road (now moved to Kings Cross) but before long decanted into neighbouring buildings. Pip and I found ourselves in a café around the corner in Old Compton Street, where we drank *grappa* and small cups of strong Italian coffee – *espresso*, but we did not know the name then. One of the students (I think he was

Italian or Spanish) said that he lived next door to the café and had lost his cat. Would I go and help him find it? Despite an air of *savoir-faire*, I was a fairly naïve youth with insipid looks and I agreed to go with him. We went next door and up a series of flights of stairs to an attic, where I was told we could get on to the roof and look for the cat. I took all this at face value until, in the process of climbing out of the window, I felt a hand on my rump. "No, no," I said. "You misunderstand. I'm not in the least homosexual. In fact, I like women very much." Surprisingly, that was that. The Italian (or Spaniard) apologised, we returned to the café and Pip and I soon went home.

At seventeen years of age, my experience of women was minimal – and my knowledge of anything to do with sex even less so. Lower down the school, we did have biology lessons but I cannot remember them involving methods of reproduction – "the birds and the bees", as it was then referred to – and certainly not anything about human reproduction. In fact, I did not fully understand how I had come into the world until I was at Oxford and a girl-friend, who was a midwife, dragged me into a cinema to see the film, *How a Baby is Born*. Our main opportunity at Highbury for meeting the opposite sex was the weekly dance class – fraternising at other times was discouraged and two masters used to patrol Highbury Fields at lunchtime in summer to make sure that boys did not mix with the girls from Highbury Hill. The dance classes were highly structured, formal affairs, run by a couple who had had a son at the school at some time or other. Here we were taught the Waltz, Quick-Step, Foxtrot and – for those really advanced and with a committed dance partner – the gyrations and bends of the Tango. Once we had mastered the steps and holds of these various 'modern' dances, we were encouraged to put them into practice at monthly dances. These were held on Saturday evenings in the school hall, with a band instead of gramophone records. It was only at these monthly dances that we dared to experiment with 'jive', since the dance master was totally against any rhythmic movements which did not involve the couple decorously holding on to each other for the duration. However, the pop music of the time was already encouraging us to jive and swing. This was long before the Beatles and the Rolling Stones, even before

Elvis Presley – Bill Hayley and *Rock Around the Clock* only became top of the charts in America in July 1955. The popular music of the time (not then known as 'pop') came from Chris Barber, Ken Colyer and Lonnie Donegan, who with a washboard and guitar provided a form of easy jazz known as 'skiffle'.

The age of skiffle saw a loosening up of dress codes for the first time since the war. The changes were spearheaded by Teddy Boys, who sported long jackets, drainpipe trousers and crêpe-soled shoes, known as 'brothel creepers', and had their hair sleeked back in a quiff or pompadour hairstyle. Until then, male hair styles had been remarkably conservative – few men had long hair and the 'short back and sides' given to recruits in the Army was only an exaggeration of what we all had at school. No one had shaved heads: that was the badge of shame, given to Nazi collaborators in France. I did not become a Teddy Boy (there were only a few at Highbury) but I did buy a bright tweed jacket, slim trousers, a coloured tie and a pair of crêpe-soled shoes and proudly sported this new gear at school dances. It was a change to be proud of. Until then I had dressed in hand-me-down clothes, including a striped suit of Dad's – my first 'long trousers' at the age of 13.

The opportunity to buy a new rig came from my increased income in 1952-53. In addition to my paper round, I was now working on Saturdays cleaning and maintaining sewing machines for a rag-trade manufacturer, Alec D. Kisberg, who had a small factory behind his shop at the corner of Almeida Street and Upper Street (now a classy restaurant). Mum probably made the introduction as she had done out-work for Kisberg, sewing on buttons. My work was messy – I had to scrape oil-soaked thread and fluff from the machine's innards – but well paid. Kisberg paid me a pound per Saturday, and extra if I washed and waxed his car. Before I finally left school, he gave me an expensive shirt and tie.

The girls who came to the monthly dances were present or past pupils of Highbury Hill. One of them was a small blonde with a ponytail, named Marion. I think I danced with her only once but was so besotted that I wrote her name a hundred times on the cover of an exercise book. A more communicative young woman was Jean

McCrindle, daughter of the actor Alex McCrindle, famous to us as 'Jock' in the radio soap, *Dick Barton, Special Agent* – he later appeared as General Dodonna in the first *Star Wars* film. Jean was a friend with whom we were well able to chat – in fact she later became a prominent left-wing academic – but she was also very fit and training in ballet. I put my life in her hands when we jived.

My regular dancing partner and first real girlfriend was Pat Barnes. We had more in common than an ability to get round the floor together in the Quick Step, since she was Deputy Head Girl at Highbury Hill while I was Head Boy of Highbury County. We both belonged to a small madrigal choir drawn from the two schools. She lived in Riversdale Road, off Blackstock Road, and as we became better acquainted I would lie in wait for her at Highbury Barn and offer to carry her books home. But the ruse did not succeed for long. Pat was a serious young woman, hoping to go to London University to study chemistry, and inclined to look on romantic gestures as silly and unnecessary. We seldom held hands and our good-night kisses under the shadow of a tree opposite her house were no more than chaste brushing of the lips. In place of romance, we spent our time together talking about science, life and religion since at the time Pat attended Christ Church, Highbury, but was inclined to call herself an atheist. We spent quite a bit of time in each other's company – walking, going to the cinema or concerts and listening to long-play records. There was no record player in our flat, so I was pleased at Pat's house to hear a whole Beethoven piano concerto played on a stack of vinyl 78's, balanced on the auto-change of her father's record player. Her father was 'in the print', a compositor or linotype operator at the *Daily Express* and thus one of the élite of Fleet Street. I don't think he approved of me, though I got on well with her brother who had been at Highbury and followed his father into a print apprenticeship. My Mum liked Pat and had long-term expectations of our relationship. However, Pat and I parted when I left to do National Service and she went to university. She then wrote me a touching and rather humbling letter in which she thanked me for my "principles".

The new Headmaster, R.J. King (left) with Mrs Cobbie (school secretary), L. Lincoln (Latin), Charlie Garrett (History), E.G. Taylor (Divinity) and E.S. Wood (English).

The new Headmaster

At the beginning of my second year in the Sixth, there was a change of Headmaster. Mr R.J. Marsh, the rotund and avuncular head who had steered the school through wartime evacuation and post-war recovery, retired and was replaced by Mr R.J. King. King was an active Congregationalist – a member of the denomination that later joined up with the Presbyterians to form the United Reformed Church. This did not make him popular among the younger teachers, though the old hands took the change in their stride.

One of Mr King's first acts was to make me Head Boy, which was a total surprise to me and everyone else. I was not the obvious candidate – Zvi Jagendorf was intellectually more qualified and Patrick Ashton, a superb athlete who was hoping to read Medicine at Cambridge, was better qualified than either of us. Besides, I had a record in the lower school of being a prankster who had been caned frequently. It was my religious interests that probably counted with Mr King. Being Head Boy was fun. Zvi was my deputy and, wearing short gowns like the 'bum-freezers' worn by students at Oxford, we would lord it over the other prefects who were all friends and contemporaries. There was no public school 'fagging' and we had no powers to impose punishments on anyone. But we did found a school magazine and allowed ourselves unofficial 'away days' at the Law Courts and Parliament.

In those days it was the custom for pupils at public schools and grant-aided grammar schools to spend a third year in the Sixth Form after taking A levels so that they could gain a university place at Oxford or Cambridge. The practice was almost totally unknown in state grammar schools like Highbury County. And there was no UCAS or clearing house for university places at that time. One applied direct to the university or universities of one's choice, if possible on the advice and with the guidance of graduate teachers at school. It was from Zvi, I think, that I first got the idea of going to Oxbridge – he was applying to read English at Wadham College. It was obvious that, if I gained a place, I too would be reading English. Mr King advised me not to study Theology for a first degree, even though at the time I was contemplating ordination as a Vicar in the Church of England. But which colleges should I apply to?

As I was still keen on singing (and had a good alto or counter-tenor voice), I got the notion into my head that I might make it as a choral scholar if I first gained a place at either King's College, Cambridge, or New College, Oxford – the two colleges with the most famous choirs. And so I entered my name for an open scholarship in English at each and duly sat the two exams. That was not at all the way that schoolboys won choral scholarships – which entailed a music exam and voice test – but nobody told me that. All I can remember of the Oxford exam is the interview that followed it, conducted with great jollity by two college tutors, Lord David Cecil and John Bayley (later husband of the novelist, Iris Murdoch).

The Cambridge exam was a far more intimidating affair. It was held in early January 1956, when snow lay thick on the ground, and I was given accommodation in a tall-ceilinged room in the classical Gibb Building of King's. The quietness matched the coldness of the room: the only sound was the distant playing of a harpsichord, probably by the college organist, Boris Ord. As soon as I went down to breakfast the next morning, I realised what a huge mistake I had made. The dining room resonated with the clipped accents of public

Three of the Highbury Sixth Form – Herbert (Zvi) Jagendorf left, Pat Ashton and the author – from a 1953 Panoramic photograph of the whole school.

school boys – only boys of course, because the main colleges of Cambridge and Oxford did not then admit women. My competitors in that examination were Etonians, Wykhamists (from Winchester College) and Harrovians.

Back in London, I despaired of the exams I had taken and wrote letters to every Oxford college, telling them that I hoped to get good A level grades and seeking a place. Surprisingly, I was offered places to read Theology at two colleges and a place to study agriculture at a third. In the event, New College offered me a place on the strength of the scholarship exam – I am convinced that it was my pen portrait of Mr Lincoln with his winged collar and hobnail boots that clinched it. Just as well, for my A level results were not as good as I had hoped. In English I gained a Distinction (75 per cent) and in Latin 60 per cent, but in French I managed only an Ordinary level pass, even though my overall mark was 57 per cent and the pass was 40 per cent. I had misread the instructions and missed out a mandatory question. Mum said it was because I had had a row with Pat Barnes the night before, but I think it was just carelessness.

While revising for the French exam I used to get up a little earlier for my paper-round and try to read at least one page of the copy of *Le Monde*, which I was meant to deliver in Canonbury Place, behind the Tower Theatre. The owner was Raymond Mortimer, the chief book reviewer for the *Sunday Times* and a well-known francophile. One morning he came out and told me he didn't object to my reading his paper but would I – please – try to fold it correctly.

A trip to Canada

I was due to leave school in July 1956 and start National Service in the Army in September, but Mr King had another surprise for me – I really was his favoured son (he had only a daughter). The surprise was a scholarship for a fortnight's tour of Eastern Canada. The scholarships were provided by Mr W.H. Rhodes, a Bradford wool merchant and laundry king (he guaranteed the return of clean overalls within 24 hours, though not necessarily one's own) for six grammar school boys each from Bradford, Birmingham, Glasgow and London. And so in early August I met some of the other lucky scholars and we travelled to Liverpool, where we embarked on the 20,000 ton Cunard liner, RMS Franconia. The voyage to Quebec took five days and we spent much of the time showing off to each other – as teenage boys do – and to the girls on board who seemed more interested in us than in National Service RAF officers going to Canada for pilot training. In Quebec we were shown the Heights of Abraham, which General Wolfe daringly captured from the French in 1759, and given a civic reception. More receptions followed in Montreal, Ottawa, Toronto and Hamilton, all of which we reached by motor coach, sometimes – as in Hamilton – with a police motorcycle escort. Then back to Toronto to take a night train to North Bay in northern Ontario and a coach to Camp Wanapitei on Lake Temagami. Our stay there for four days, surrounded by pine forests, was idyllic. We did all the things that Cockneys or Glaswegians had only read about in the novels of Jack London – canoeing, swimming in the lake, hiking through dense undergrowth, cooking over a log fire, singing late into the night. The presence of a similar sized party of American Girl Scouts added to the delights of the place. Then coach and train to Quebec and the RMS Saxonia back to Liverpool with memories and souvenirs of a splendid holiday. Only two weeks later, I had to report to a barracks in Aldershot for the beginning of National Service.

Religion

Before leaving my schooldays, I need to say something about my attitude towards religion. This is a difficult subject. While descriptions of Islington in the nineteen-fifties or life in a London grammar school may strike a chord with the younger generation, the activities of being a choir boy and altar server may seem like something from a bygone age – Victorian maybe, like something from the *Barchester Chronicles*. But the fact is that for seven or eight years, I did nurse the intention – it may even have been a vocation – of being ordained as a priest in the Church of England.

What happened to me in 1953-54 to make me religious? First of all there was my upbringing. Mum and Dad were firm and quite literal believers in the Gospels – Mum especially so. She had a simple yet deep and unshakeable conviction that Jesus Christ's death on the cross made him her personal Saviour, a belief she shared with Dad since they had first met at the Moreland Street mission. They were what we would today term 'born again Christians', like their fellow worshippers at the Chorley Hall Mission who Sunday after Sunday stood up at the front and gave witness or 'testimony' (as they called it) as to when, where and how they had been 'saved'. Some of them knew the time to the nearest minute. And their fellow evangelicals would shout 'Amen' and 'Hallelujah'. My parents were not ostentatious like that but they did believe in personal salvation.

I did flirt with having a religious conversion, of being 'saved'. That was something my family seemed to expect, especially Mum. So when the American evangelist Billy Graham was planning his Greater London Crusade in the 1950s, I went to one of the preliminary meetings, held in a marquee on a bomb site near Highbury Corner, and may even have gone to the front to declare my willingness to be saved. Unlike modern American television evangelists, such as Jerry Falwell or Pat Robertson, Graham was apolitical – even though the Labour Party tried to stop him coming to Britain because one of his staff had attacked "the woes brought about by Socialism". I would not have disagreed at that time of austerity. In March 1954 I went to one of the Crusade meetings held in the Harringay arena (where I had been previously for the Harringay Racers motorbike speedway). It was quite an experience – huge crowds of people, an organ playing hymns as if they were swing tunes, a crooner and massed choirs rhythmically singing: "This is my Story, this is my Song, praising my Saviour all the day long ..." Then Billy Graham's invitation, pressed home again and again in the ensuing silences, for members of the audience to go forward and "declare yourself for Jesus". It would have taken a more resolute cynic than I to resist. So I went with hundreds of others and was taken aside and counselled by an evangelical volunteer who asked if I had any existing church connection. And of course I had – at Christ Church, West Green, Tottenham.

I had gone to Tottenham as a choir boy and remained just that, until the arrival of a new vicar who was keen to see as many of the boys as possible confirmed. So I went to confirmation classes, instructed in the antiquated questions and answers of the Book of Common Prayer Catechism, and was confirmed in 1952 by the Bishop of Willesdon. This should have been an important milestone in my life, a social event similar to the Bar Mitzvah for Jewish boys or the First Communion for Catholics. But for me it was a wholly private affair and I don't think even my parents attended.

The classes were run by the new vicar, the Rev. Lionel Gubbins, who was far from being an intellectual. In fact, he had started his working life as a dock clerk in Dublin and, after war service in the RAF, found it difficult to get accepted for ordination training because of a lack of educational qualifications. Lionel was an Anglo-Catholic and, in line with the Liturgical Movement then gaining strength in the Church of England, soon introduced a Sung Eucharist and the wearing of vestments. These changes required servers to assist the priest at the altar and I was chosen and trained to be one. So, once a month, instead of arriving late in the vestry and donning a cassock and surplice for the choir, now I had to be early and dress myself in an alb (a long white tunic), an amice (a folded sort of collar) and a cincture (girdle). These were of course similar vestments to those worn by Roman Catholic priests and servers – Mum would have been horrified if she had known what I was wearing. Lionel Gubbins was a great influence on me, not for any intellectual input but as an example of what a hard-working, prayerful and respected priest could do in a not particularly glamorous community like Tottenham. He was a bachelor and lived in a large vicarage next to the church, cooked and cleaned for by a small, genteel housekeeper, Miss Bray. The Christ Church I knew – a cavernous red-brick building – has now been demolished and replaced by flats with a smaller, modern church built nearby

The other influence on me was very different. He was the Rev. E.G. Taylor – mentioned earlier – the Divinity (RI) teacher at Highbury, also the choirmaster and indefatigable organiser of summer camps. EG was not an Anglo-Catholic and certainly not an Evangelical: he was what we would now call a Liberal theologian, though at that time the term was not widely used. I remember in one lesson when, referring to Jesus walking on the water of the Sea of Galilee, he suggested that there were sandbanks just below the surface and the important point of the story was the gullibility of the Apostles. He had just finished this explanation when a boy at the front of the class asked: "'Ere, Sir, couldn't it 'a bin a miracle?" When I was in the Sixth Form, EG gave me informal tutorials on the New Testament. It was from him that I understood there were theological as well as historical differences in the narratives told by Matthew, Mark, Luke and John and the earliest – and probably historically the most trustworthy as history – was Mark. He introduced me to modern biblical criticism and, particularly, to the work of one of his heroes, Albert Schweitzer – the philosopher, theologian, organist and doctor who had set up a hospital deep in the jungle of West Africa in 1912. This included Schweitzer's ground-breaking work, *The Quest of the Historical Jesus*, in which he reviewed all former books on the 'historical Jesus' and showed that the image of Jesus had changed with the times and outlooks of the various authors.

I chose Schweitzer's *Quest* when I was awarded a school prize in 1954 and read it over and over during National Service. It was intellectually the most stimulating book I had ever come across. I had a similar liberating feeling of excitement when, many years later, I read *Jesus of Nazareth* by Joseph Klausner, who wrote that Jesus was best understood as a Jew who was trying to reform his own religion, not to create another one – and he died as a devout Jew.

The Rev. E.G. Taylor (left) and his hero, Albert Schweitzer.

Klausner was the great-uncle of the Israeli novelist, Amos Oz.

So, aged eighteen and about to leave school, I had a nuanced and somewhat contradictory – if not confused – attitude to religion. On the one hand, I was a confirmed member of the Church of England, an altar server in the Catholic tradition and pointed in the direction of becoming a priest and pastor like my mentor, Lionel Gubbins. On the other hand, I was gaining a knowledge of the radical thinking among theologians, who questioned whether Jesus was born of a virgin mother in Bethlehem (or was he from an ordinary Jewish family in Nazareth), whether he intended his followers to be Christians or to remain Jews and, indeed, whether he was the 'Son of God'. They were contrasted attitudes which I put on the back burner until five years later, at theological college.

What surprises me, looking back over sixty years, is my (indeed *our*) lack of interest in politics. The Conservative Party was firmly in power at Westminster, the Labour Party seemed moribund after its defeat in the 1951 election and – despite my feelings of alienation among the public school boys at the Cambridge scholarship exam – I was not a 'class warrior'. If only I could have had a cause. Zvi Jagendorf had a cause: as a 'Zionist' he intended to move to the new State of Israel as soon as was practical. But my only cause was religion. Much later there were many causes on offer, including protesting against nuclear weapons – 'Ban the Bomb'.

9.
Before leaving Islington

In September 1954 I became a soldier. The reason was National Service which at that time every boy of eighteen had to do. It meant two years in the Army, Royal Navy or Royal Air Force, unless he was exempt for health or a few other reasons, like training to be a doctor. At first I found it an enormous shock, physically and psychologically. There were the early mornings (Reveille at 6 am), the daily inspections of one's kit which had to be laid out according to a set pattern, the drill and the marching up and down the parade ground, the horror of having some sergeant shouting orders all the time, and so on ... Basic training was done at Aldershot where we were housed in barrack rooms which had toilets that did not work – and yet we had to clean them all the same. Willems Barracks (named after a British victory against Napoleon) had open verandahs like Sing-Sing prison and were condemned for cavalry use in 1938 – but were still used by the RASC (Royal Army Service Corps) until 1964. A Tesco superstore now occupies the site.

My memories of that period are summed up in an incident at breakfast. Each soldier was issued with two china plates which had to be cleaned in a big trough of boiling hot water outside the 'cookhouse'. After supper, the water would be too dirty to clean the plates properly, so it was usually a good idea to wisk them up and down in clean water before breakfast. Unfortunately, one day I was jostled by other soldiers and lost my grip on one of the plates. As a result, I had to have all my breakfast on the other plate – fried egg, baked beans, sausage, followed by bread, butter and jam – all dolloped on with gusto by the cooks. Then I had to wait for the water in the trough to cool before I could retrieve the first plate.

After the shocks of basic training, we were asked to choose a trade. I said I wanted to be a driver or a boatman or a baker or a cook, but was told: 'No, you will be a clerk'. Realising that that could be a very boring occupation, I applied to become an officer. After all, officers received extra pay and had a more comfortable (or as we called it 'cushy') life in the officers' mess. I went to what was called a WOSBY (War Office Selection Board) and was assigned various tasks, like organising a platoon of six soldiers to cross a river with the aid of a short plank, a barrel and a length of rope (which I did successfully). There were also interviews. In one interview, which I remember very clearly, a fierce colonel from an infantry regiment said that he did not think I was 'officer material'. He said I came from Islington, which he had heard was a very rough area. With my fingers crossed, I then told a little lie: "actually, Sir, it is Canonbury". He said that that was even rougher. He then ended the interview by saying that I was a young man who had done very well for himself, including getting a place at a college of Oxford University – "I think you have gone far enough for the time being: You are not the sort of person who will fit into an officers' mess".

So, I went back to training as an Army clerk and learned to type. After the training, I was asked if I wanted a posting at home or abroad. Feeling adventurous, I answered 'abroad'. That could have meant going to Singapore and Malaya, where the Army was engaged in an 'emergency' fighting Communist guerrillas, or to Cyprus where there was also trouble from 'Eoka' guerillas. In fact, I was posted to Germany to a garrison in a small town called Sennelager.

Germany in the 1950s was split between east and west and still occupied by the nations which had defeated Hitler's *Wehrmacht* in 1945. West Germany was divided into the American, French and British zones – Sennelager was in the British zone – and had recently become the Federal Republic of Germany (*Bundesrepublik Deutschland*). East Germany was occupied by the Soviet Union (the Russian Communist state) and had formed itself into the German Democratic Republic (*Deutsche Demokratische Republik*). The former German capital, Berlin, was similarly divided and in 1948 the Russians blocked the allies' rail and road access to their sectors, which was only alleviated by the 'Berlin airlift' of thousands of supply flights. This confrontation was part of the so-called 'Cold War', when the British government and its allies formed themselves into the North Atlantic Treaty Organisation (NATO) so as to be ready if the Russians decided to attack West Germany. There was also the growing threat of a nuclear confrontation between NATO and the Soviet Union and its communist allies.

Because there is a huge area of heathland behind the Sennelager camp, its main use to the British Army and NATO was exercises in tank warfare, but it did provide room for other, less aggressive activities. One of these was a centre for training clerks in the administration and paperwork of the fighting units. This meant chiefly drawing up 'Operation Orders', the blueprints for launching an attack upon the enemy (or a retreat, for that matter). Operation Orders followed a rigid pattern of sections and sub-sections, and were phrased in the abbreviated English so beloved of the military, and particularly of the NATO alliance. So, having ascertained through *MI* and *sigint* (military and signals intelligence) that *Redforce* (the Russians) was engaged in *M&T* (movement and transport), *COMOPS* (the commander of operations) might order an *ECR, Movsumrep* and *geositrep* (an enemy contact report, a movement summary report and a geographic situation report). It was like learning a foreign language. And there was also the new NATO alphabet to be learned amd rigorously followed: A for ALFA, B for BRAVO, C for CHARLIE, D for DELTA, E for ECHO, F for FOXTROT, G for GOLF and so on. Woe betide anyone referring to A for Apple or B for Bertie.

So this was the additional training we were to undergo for our first month in Germany. It was run by a group of sergeants and corporals, who were all National Servicemen like us, under the overall command of a Captain Norris. Softly spoken and a devout Roman Catholic, Norris would come up behind the drill sergeants on the parade ground (we still did square-bashing) and tell them most politely that on no account were they to swear when they shouted their commands. This left the drill sergeants completely tongue-tied. I was made an instructor and promoted to corporal and, eventually, to sergeant – but I never took a parade, with or without swearing.

Teaching Operation Orders to intake after intake of National Servicemen – a month at a time – was a boring business. In compensation, I took a correspondence course in Economics and Industrial Relations with Ruskin College, Oxford. I should have spent time learning German, but people in that part of Germany spoke

Sergeant Perman outside the classrooms of the
All Arms Training Centre at Sennelager in 1956.

Low German. I should also have explored Germany more than I did. I regret never having visited Berlin while it was still divided between East and West and one had to cross at Checkpoint Charlie. But I did visit towns in the immediate area of Sennelager – Bielefeld and Paderborn, where I attended a memorable performance of Bach's *St. John Passion.*

With a growing sense of detachment, I observed the idiocies of a large peacetime army, reliant on thousands of reluctant school-leavers, which had not adjusted to life in postwar Europe. During 1955, the allies were planning the creation of a West German army (the *Bundeswehr*) under a treaty arrangement called the West European Union. The papers for this came to our offices in the Sennelager garrison and were marked *NATO TOP SECRET.* I found them one morning laid out on a desk where Yogoslav cleaners had been working an hour earlier. Another thing which I found amusing was our sergeant-major's practice of standing rigidly to attention when he answered a telephone call from an officer.

Despite my easy life as a sergeant, I looked forward eagerly to being 'demobbed' in September 1956. But, just then, the international situation became heated and our life in Sennelager became more interesting. The main reason for this was the Suez Crisis. In July 1956, President Gamal Abdul Nasser of Egypt had nationalised the Suez Canal, the vital trade route between Europe and Asia, and plans were made in secret by the British, French and Israeli governments to invade Egypt to win back the canal and overthrow Nasser. The Israelis invaded first, followed quickly by British and French units. In Sennelager, we saw the arrival of army reservists who had been demobbed a few months earlier, while some of the tank units left for the Hamburg docks in expectation of all-out war. In the event, the whole thing turned out to be a costly and humiliating failure, in which the United States sided with Russia and other powers to force the British and French to withdraw, while Nasser remained in power and gained in popularity. As a result, Britain's position as a leading world power was seriously compromised.

Another result of the Suez affair was that the Soviet Union used it as a smoke-screen for putting down a revolt against Communist rule in Hungary. Israeli paratroops invaded Egypt on 29 October, Russian tanks moved into Hungary on 23 October. Six weeks earlier, waiting to be demobbed, I remember standing in a food queue, reading a long newspaper analysis of the Hungarian crisis and the courageous stand of the liberal-minded Prime Minister, Imre Nagy. I was leaving the army and the world was changing more rapidly than at any time since 1945.

I was now a civilian again but I was not to return to Lewis Buildings or Islington – my family had now moved to Hemel Hempstead in Hertfordshire. Despairing of ever getting a house while on the London County Council list, Mum had persuaded Dad to apply for an engineering job in Hemel, a job that involved night work and months of commuting before they were allocated a new terraced house in the New Town. Much to my parents' joy, it had a long back garden. Hemel Hempstead was now my home. So I was no longer an Islington boy from Lewis Buildings. My Islington childhood had come to an end.